HARRIETT PRESS

BUCKLE DOWN

HOW I INVENTED SOUTH KOREA'S FIRST AUTOMOBILE ENGINE

DR. HYUN-SOON LEE
translated by Hannah Pang

About the Author

Dr Hyun-Soon Lee is currently the vice chairman and chief technology officer of the Doosan Group. He received his MA and PhD in mechanical engineering from the State University of New York at Stony Brook. He began his professional career at the General Motors Research Institute before leaving to join Hyundai in 1984. During his career with Hyundai, Dr Lee was instrumental in developing the first engine produced by Hyundai, also known as the Alpha engine, and in the development of the Beta engine.

He has received numerous awards for his contributions to the automobile industry, including the IR52 Jang Young Shil Prize from South Korea's Ministry of Science and Technology, and the Gold Medal for Anti-Pollution Technology Development from the South Korean newspaper *Chosun Ilbo*. For his leadership, he was awarded the Best Chief Technology Officer award by the Korea Industrial Technology Association. Dr Lee is a member of the Presidential Advisory Council on Science and Technology and the National Academy of Engineering in South Korea. He lives in Seoul, South Korea.

About the Translator

Hannah Pang received her BA in geography from the National University of Singapore, and her MA in international studies from Korea University in Seoul, South Korea. She has received a translation grant from the Literature Translation Institute of Korea to translate South Korean poet Tae-Jun Moon's poetry collection *A Faraway Place*. Her translations have been published in *The Guardian*. Her translations include Jim Kim's *Grab and Go: A Food Business Millionaire's Secrets to Achieving What He Wants in Life* (Harriett Press).

Harriett Press Pte Ltd
Telepark 5 Tampines Central 6
#03-38 Singapore 529482
harriettpress.com

Copyright © 2014 by Hyun-Soon Lee.
English translation © 2020 by Hannah Pang.
All rights reserved.

Originally published in Korean under the title Wake Up Your Sleeping Engine. This English edition is published by arrangement with Gimm-Young Publishers, Inc. through Duran Kim Agency. This book is published with the support of the Literature Translation Institute of Korea (LTI Korea).

No part of this publication may be reproduced, distributed, stored in a retrieval system or transmitted in any form or by any means – electronic, mechanical, photocopy, recording, scanning or other – except for brief quotations for the purpose of criticism and review, without the prior written permission of the publisher.

All photographs and illustrations are courtesy of the author.

Printed in Singapore

National Library Board, Singapore Cataloguing-in-Publication Data
Names: Lee, Hyun-Soon. | Pang, Hannah, translator.
Title: Buckle down: how I invented South Korea's first automobile engine / Dr. Hyun-Soon Lee; translated by Hannah Pang.
Description: Singapore: Harriett Press Pte Ltd, [2020] | Translated from Korean.
Identifiers: OCN 1151698630 | ISBN 978-981-14-4951-2 (paperback) | 978-981-14-4952-9 (e-book)
Subjects: LCSH: Lee, Hyun-Soon. | Automobile engineers--Korea (South)--Biography. | Automobiles--Korea (South)--Design and construction.
Classification: DDC 629.2092--dc23

Our titles may be purchased in bulk for business, promotional or educational use. For more information, please email editor@harriettpress.com.

Contents

Foreword	1
Prologue	4
Part 1 – 'What Will I Do?' Versus 'How Will I Live?'	9
1 A Child Who Grew Up Amid the Ravages of War	11
2 The Stubbornest Child in the World	14
3 I Couldn't Defeat My Father's Obstinacy	18
4 My First Setback in Middle School	21
5 'What Will I Do?' Versus 'How Will I Live?'	26
6 In Everything, Foundation First	28
7 South Korea Is Too Small for Me	30
Part 2 – Just Follow Your Heart	33
8 Learn from the Best	35
9 Getting an A Without Sitting the Test	40
10 I'll Teach *You*, Professor	42
11 Standing at a Crossroads	48
12 Nothing Is Impossible	52
13 That Guy Is a Con Artist	56
14 Dr Lee, What Did You Come Here to Do?	61
Part 3 – Starting Work in a Technology Wasteland	65
15 The Best Begin with Their Sights Set on the Future	67
16 Foes or Allies?	71
17 Should I Just Give Up?	75

18	Mitsubishi Offers to Reduce Its Royalties by Half	80
19	I Shall Learn Despite Every Form of Humiliation	84
20	We Do Not Work with a Third-Rate Company	87
21	Building a Gearbox Independently Too	92

Part 4 – Inventing South Korea's First Automobile Engine   95

22	Why Does the Engine Keep Falling Apart?	97
23	Oh, Eureka!	101
24	Failure Is Simply the Road to Success	104
25	The Jang Yeong Shil Award and Hospitalisation	107
26	Even Chairman Kubo Gave Us Recognition	111
27	We Want to Partner with Hyundai	114
28	The Misfortunate Gamma Engine	118
29	Finally, Royalties!	122
30	Welcome, Dr Lee – Father of the World Engine!	129
31	Why Can't You Make Electric Vehicles?	135
32	Without Our Own Technology	139

Part 5 – Driving the World with My Own Technology   143

33	Now Let's Defeat Them Using Technology	145
34	Beautiful Days of My Life	148
35	Teamwork That Transforms Crises into Opportunities	152
36	More Terrifying Than an Enraged Superior	158
37	My Special Mode of Communication	161
38	Achieving Miracles with One Heart and Mind	164
39	No Eternal Victor in the World of Technology	168

Epilogue   172

Foreword

The Passionate Mentor We've Been Waiting for

The faces of the students I meet when I stroll around the university campus are generally depressed and dark. They have their hands full, busily studying and building up their specs.[1] As a professor and an alumnus of the university, my heart is ill at ease when I see them. I'm also bustling about these days, just like the students, trying to offer them help, however little.

I love cars. When I studied abroad in the United States thirty-five years ago, I saw cars that could take me wherever I wanted to go, and I fell for them head over heels. Eventually, I resigned from the electrical and electronics company I was happily working at and moved to an automobile company. Everyone told me that I was mad. Hardly anyone leaves California, which is apparently the best place to live in America, for barren and desolate Detroit. But that was how infatuated I was with cars.

---

1 Translator's note – 'Specs' is short for 'specifications', a relatively new term coined in South Korea to refer to a person's qualifications and skills, such as their academic grades, foreign-language test scores, work experience and volunteering activities.

Dr Hyun-Soon Lee, the author of this book, is someone who loves cars as much as I do. More accurately, he is someone who is fanatical about automobile engines. General Motors, a global automobile company, promised him not only an environment where he could research engines as much as he liked, but also a high salary and stable company benefits. However, he gave them all up and returned to South Korea. Why did he make such a rash decision?

It was Dr Lee who invented South Korea's very first automobile engine. In the 1980s, when he started developing automobile engines, nobody thought that South Korea possessed the technical skills to construct automobile engines. But he embraced the lofty dream that South Korea could do it too, and he took up the challenge. If not for his resolve and his rise to the challenge to stop the country from further relying on overseas technology, South Korea would not have seen the development of its current automobile industry.

Young people now need the time to examine themselves first, rather than build up their specs. Right now, let's think seriously, starting with what we love doing most. Life expectancy is gradually increasing, and we will live to be well over a hundred years old in future, so young people need time to mull over the kind of careers they want and the lives they will lead over a hundred years. And the way they build up that career must stand out from others. It's difficult to succeed by following in the footsteps of others, or of one's seniors. What's effortless for me will be effortless for others too, and what's onerous for me will be onerous for others too. Ultimately, it's a far more valuable feat to achieve what's onerous and impossible for others.

Foreword

It's said that the happiest people in the world are people who do what they love. I have never had a boring day researching automobiles. It was the same for Dr Lee too. It was a path that others hadn't trodden because they had thought it was impossible, but he set forth with perseverance and a heart that adored cars, and in the end he realised his dream. This book is a record of his passion and his perspiration. I believe there is no better mentor for future engineers who are undecided on the direction of their career. And I'm certain that this book will serve as a signpost to young people who have yet to find their paths in life.

Professor Myeong-Ho Seonwoo
Director of Automotive Control and Electronics Laboratory,
Department of Automotive Engineering, Hanyang University

Prologue

To Young People Living in an Age of Mental Poverty

In the spring of 1984, I arrived at Gimpo Airport with great ambitions. It was eight years since I had left for the United States to study engine technology. Up until that point, I had completed postgraduate study and then worked as an automobile engine researcher at General Motors (GM).

The late chairman of the Hyundai Group, Ju-Yung Chung, had yearned more than anyone else to develop an engine – the high spot and heart of automobile technology – using South Korean technology. And for a long time, he had been trying to persuade me to develop an automobile engine together with him. In the end, I decided to join Hyundai Motors and resigned from GM. My superior at GM, who received my resignation letter, spared no effort to stop me leaving. He told me that no matter how hard I worked at a latecomer company like Hyundai Motors, I would never catch up with a developed automobile company like GM.[2] I didn't

---

[2] Translator's note – Hyundai Motors was founded in South Korea in December 1967; General Motors started in the United States in September 1908.

change my mind, because as an engineer I had great ambitions and confidence in my own technical skills.

But I can still vividly recall my feelings of helplessness when I reported for work at Hyundai Motors for the first time. At that time, all Chairman Chung did was simply introduce five subordinates to me. My salary had been reduced to one third of what I had received at GM. Even the building construction for the engine development research institute had not begun. I had enjoyed material benefits and the freedom to conduct as much research as I desired at GM; by comparison, the environment at Hyundai Motors was indescribably inadequate. But I didn't mind. If I had minded, I wouldn't have returned to South Korea in the first place.

My mind was occupied with just one goal: the dream of developing an automobile engine with my own hands! It was a challenge that was worth an adamant young engineer risking his life. Without this dream, I would not have abandoned a decent job that had been the envy of others to return to South Korea.

But my life at Hyundai Motors was never plain sailing. That we had to start everything from scratch wasn't a problem. The largest barrier I faced at Hyundai Motors was the deep-seated stereotypes that people who worked there held. They harboured a sense of defeat, believing that we could never develop engines with our own technology, and they had a lackadaisical attitude according to which they intended to rely on advanced technologies from abroad, rather than having the tenacity to succeed with the technology they had themselves.

On my first day at work, my direct superior drove me into a corner.

"About that engine you said you were going to develop, I don't think it's going to work. I've no idea what you're thinking of, coming all the way here!"

His face was filled with suspicion and mistrust.

Even back then, there was hardly anyone at Hyundai Motors who believed that we could develop engines by our own strength. And not without reason. Up until then, Hyundai Motors had never created an engine independently. In those days, Hyundai Motors purchased engine technology from abroad, and simply assembled car parts before exporting the finished products. The board of directors was deeply worried that the fact that we were developing our own engine might inadvertently become known abroad. There were even people who accused me of being a con artist.

"Creating our own engine sounds good, but how are we going to create an engine that even Mitsubishi finds difficult to manufacture? If a young and inexperienced person decides to con other people, he should at least do it within limits!"

They denigrated me whenever they had the opportunity, and they obstructed my engine development project.

I hadn't expected rousing cheers. But the fears and stereotypes of the engineers, who had never once had any confidence in technological development, were more rigid than I had expected. I had to first break down that barrier. The only way to break down that barrier was to build our own engine by our own strength.

Looking back, my life has been a series of challenges. I've always risen to the challenge of projects that had no more than a twenty or thirty percent chance of success. When I was studying abroad in the United States thirty-eight years ago, South Korea was an

Prologue

impoverished country with nothing it could show off to the world. If I hadn't been awarded a scholarship from the State University of New York, it would have been difficult to even dream of studying abroad. I have come so far, in a country where everything was ravaged by war, because I had a bold spirit that sought to become the world's best engineer.

It was the same when I was developing automobile engines. I believed that we certainly ought to build engines with our own hands if we were a company that manufactured automobiles. I was also prideful, wanting to accomplish for myself what everyone else considered impossible to achieve. We could build our own engines, thanks to an engineer's bold spirit.

When I decided to write this book, I was worried that my story might sound like the success story of an engineer from the olden days. Now that Hyundai Motors's status and technology level have been transformed beyond recognition, I'm well aware that what I experienced as a first-generation engineer thirty years ago will not be congruous with the environment where the young generation find themselves now.

All my life I've trodden the path of an engineer. Thirty years ago, I was a mere young engineer buoyed up by his dream to develop our very own technology. I discovered new possibilities when everyone said it couldn't work, I didn't give up, and I fearlessly embraced challenges even when I failed repeatedly. That was all I knew, but I'm certain that though times have changed and technological standards have evolved, the self-cultivation that engineers need, both then and now, stays the same.

Even now, I think of my time at Hyundai Motors, which I spent facing down obstacles from rival companies and developing our own engines, as the golden days of my life. The days when my hands were black with grease, and when the other engineers and I went through thick and thin together, were the brightest days of my life.

I hope to share these experiences through this book. It chronicles the adventures of the first-generation engineers who stood tall in the global market with their own technologies, competing with engineers from developed countries who were full of themselves. My only hope is that through my story, young people, who now live in an age of material abundance but mental poverty, will become transfused with the bold spirit that is needed in this generation.

Part 1

'What Will I Do?' Versus 'How Will I Live?'

Whether I went to medical school or engineering school, I wished to expand my abilities as much as I could. Therefore, once I had entered engineering school, I applied myself without hesitation to the study of engineering. I believe that anyone can achieve better-than-expected results if they place no limits on their own abilities and give their all in every decision they make.

1

A Child Who Grew Up Amid the Ravages of War

People like to ask me this question: "When did you start dreaming of becoming an engineer?"

Perhaps it's because I hold the title of 'the developer of South Korea's first automobile engine'. They used to ask me this question in the expectation that there had been something extraordinary about me in my childhood. Maybe they wanted to hear the story of a genius engineer who had loved disassembling and assembling machines since he was young. However, my childhood was not particularly remarkable or different. On the contrary, it was so harsh a period that to dream of anything was considered a luxury.

I was born the year the Korean War began. After the war had stormed through our lives and passed, I spent my childhood living amid the ravages of the war. It seemed as if things would never be restored. Back then, I could easily find abandoned, collapsed buildings in the heart of the city. Children of my age in those days accepted such an environment as a given while they were growing up. The tragedy of a fratricidal war and the post-war restoration work all belonged to the adults' world. We were simply busy going from place to place in the fallen city, as if those places were our playgrounds, and looking for things to play with.

My very first memory of cars goes back to the mid-1950s, when I was five years old. Cars were very rare in South Korea then. It wasn't easy to spot cars in the city. It was a time when it was more commonplace to see American military jeeps, or fighter planes that would suddenly cut through the skies.

As you might expect, the first car I rode in was a jeep. An American lieutenant was living next door, and I recall that his house apparently functioned as an American military hospital. The American soldiers who frequented the hospital sometimes gave rides on the passenger seat as a favour to this hugely curious Asian boy. I was tremendously fascinated by jeeps, which raced powerfully once the ignition was turned on with a vroom. At the time, I couldn't find factory-made toys. If there were toys that we wanted, we had to make them. My two brothers and I had similar interests, so the toys we played with were also similar. We created cars by driving nails into roughly cut wooden blocks, and we built aeroplanes by cutting out and pasting paper boxes. Our toys were poorly made with clumsy workmanship, but we could play with them for an entire day, losing track of time.

When I was in elementary school, I made a crystal radio set. Crystal radios utilised semiconductor minerals to convert high-frequency signals drifting in the air into audible audio signals, and in the 1960s we could easily obtain the materials from the stationery shops outside our schools. Crystal sets were popular among kids of my age because they could be assembled relatively easily, and they produced sounds when crocodile clips were connected to the steel wires. They were a wholly different kind of toy from cars made of wood or paper planes. Though the sounds they produced were soft because of the weak signals received from the antennas, and the connection was intermittent due to their narrow reception range, they were the best toys at a time when radios were uncommon. Having personally made toys to play with, and having reflected on their operational principles while playing with them since a young age, I was naturally fearless about building things myself.

2
The Stubbornest Child in the World

I was an incredibly stubborn child. No matter what others said, I never backed down on issues that I disagreed about. The following incident took place during a science class in my fourth year of elementary school, when my teacher was explaining plant growth.

"Morning glory, like ivy, is a climber that cannot stand up and grow on its own, and it rises by climbing on other tree branches or trunks. However, interestingly, its stems twine and climb in only one direction. Can you see them twining and climbing towards the right?" my teacher said as he showed us a picture of morning glory.

As I listened attentively to the teacher, it dawned on me that something was amiss. So I raised my hand up high.

"Teacher!"

"Yes, Hyun-Soon. Do you have a question?"

"Yes. That doesn't seem right."

"What doesn't seem right?" my teacher asked again.

"What you just said. That the stems of morning glory twine towards the right."

"I did say that. And?"

"I think they seem to be twining and climbing towards the left."

My teacher then came over to my seat and explained to me kindly, "Hyun-Soon, look carefully. Do you see the stems twining from left to right?"

With his finger, he pointed at the left end of the morning glory's stems, and from there drew in the air how the stems twined and climbed upwards from left to right. As my teacher had said, the morning glory was indeed twining and climbing towards the right.

But I pointed to the right end of the stems and said, "Teacher, if you start from this side the stems twine and climb from right to left."

My teacher stared at me blankly.

"Why do you look at it from that side?"

Without backing down, I said, "Teacher, why do you look at it from *that* side?"

"What did you just say? You little rascal! How dare you talk back to your teacher!"

Frustrated, I repeated, "I'm not talking back to you. Look here, teacher. If you start from here, the stems clearly twine and climb towards the left."

Then my teacher said, as if he could no longer put up with me, "You little rascal, you just keep talking back to me, don't you? That's got to stop. Go and stand at the back of the classroom right now."

I felt wronged, but I couldn't defy my teacher, so I went and stood at the very back of the classroom. But no matter how I thought about it, I felt very wronged. I hadn't intended to oppose my teacher; I had simply told him what I had seen. I fumed alone, then burst into tears. I tried to fight back my tears, but they didn't stop.

"Hyun-Soon Lee. What reason do you have to cry? Are you going to do that again next time?"

"…"

Though I was crying, I refused to apologise. Because I didn't know what I had done wrong.

"You little rascal, you are one stubborn boy. Be careful next time."

My teacher gave a knock on my head with his knuckles and left the classroom.

When I think about it now, I can't say who was in the wrong – my teacher or me. Morning glory twines and climbs towards the right if the left is set as the starting point, as my teacher had said; and it twines and climbs towards the left if the right is set as the starting point, as I had said. In short, we can explain the same picture differently, depending on where we have set our standards.

Looking back, I see I wasn't a child who absorbed a hundred percent of what my teachers said like a sponge. Just the opposite, I was more of a child who reflected independently on whether what my teachers said was correct, and if not, why not, and I would search for the answers. During lessons too, instead of memorising them as they were, I strove to clearly understand what I was being taught, so much so that I could explain it to others. If I didn't understand something, I would inundate the teachers with questions until I did. During a physics class in high school, my interpretation of Fleming's rule differed from my teacher's explanation, so I argued with him throughout that class. Eventually, at the next class, after looking up some more material, my teacher came over to me and conceded that I was right.

Of course, it's not desirable to argue about everything for argument's sake, or to be thoughtlessly defiant. However, engineers need at least the conviction that they can push ahead to the end when they think they are right. This is because engineers are not people who imitate existing methods, but people who develop new things. When we think independently about everything, keep at it tenaciously and seek to find our own answers, instead of uncritically accepting what others say, we can improve our competence as engineers.

3
I Couldn't Defeat My Father's Obstinacy

I was born the second of three brothers. As a matter of fact, second children often find themselves in a somewhat ambiguous position in the household. The firstborn is treated well, as they are the oldest child, and the third child steals the show, as they are the youngest; but the second child doesn't enjoy such favour. It's difficult for the second child to stand out if they don't work hard on their own to distinguish themselves.

My father had extraordinary expectations, especially for my older brother. Therefore, the way he treated my older brother differed markedly from how he treated my younger brother and me. I wanted to win approval from such a father, so I did my best and worked diligently in everything I did. I was prideful, hated losing, and was satisfied only if I did exactly what my older brother was doing. I wanted to prove that I could do whatever my older brother could. I also wanted to do better than him. But it was difficult to do well and win my father's approval, because my older brother did pretty well in his studies. As a result, my goals were gradually set higher. I always set high goals that were barely achievable, and did my utmost to achieve them. It was childish now that I think about it, but this competitive spirit had

I Couldn't Defeat My Father's Obstinacy

become my motivation for studying hard. My closest brother was my fiercest competitor.

Looking back, I didn't dream of specifically becoming an engineer from childhood. But I did vaguely wish to be the best at whatever I did. I think that at crucial crossroads in my life, I have been able to make decisions I haven't come to regret because of this predisposition of mine.

During my student days, not just at university but also at middle and high school, I had to apply for the schools I wanted and sit for tests before I could be enrolled. When it came time to attend middle school, my father told me to go to Seoul Middle School. Being excellent at my studies, I had been thinking of Gyeonggi Middle School. Both were prestigious schools, but Gyeonggi Middle School was slightly better known and required high admission scores to enter. But my father thought otherwise. He continued to insist that I should attend Seoul Middle School, right up to the point when I submitted my applications.

"Mr Lee, Hyun-Soon has sufficient grades to enrol at Gyeonggi Middle School, but why do you insist on sending him to Seoul Middle School?"

My form teacher tried to dissuade my father, but he was resolute.

"I'll send my child to Seoul Middle School, why are you saying no?"

When my father couldn't persuade my form teacher, he went so far as to go to the head teacher, and he finally obtained an application form for Seoul Middle School. My pride was hugely hurt at having to attend Seoul Middle School without knowing why. Even children who had lower grades than I did had submitted applications to Gyeonggi Middle School.

"Father, I want to attend Gyeonggi Middle School too. My older brother went to Gyeonggi Middle School, why must I attend Seoul Middle School? Please send me to Gyeonggi Middle School too."

Though I was obstinate myself, I couldn't defeat my father's obstinacy. Even though it was futile no matter how much I complained, I flew into a tantrum and cried, saying I wouldn't sit the admission test. But even that didn't work on my father. In the end, I had no choice but to sit Seoul Middle School's admission test.

I found this out later, but my father wanted to send each of his three sons to a different middle school. He had sent my older brother to Gyeonggi Middle School, so he planned to send me to Seoul Middle School and my younger brother to Gyeongbok Middle School. He believed that in this way, when we three brothers set out into the world, we would have broader connections, help one another, and be capable of conducting our own social lives.

4

My First Setback in Middle School

My middle school life was smooth sailing from the outset. I was ranked second schoolwide and first in my class because of my admission scores. I had always been highly competitive and couldn't live if I lost to others, so my confidence level soared sky-high because my admission scores were good. I'd be in top of the class if I studied the way I always did, and I could play football on the school field as much as I wanted after school, because my house was nearby. When I grew bored of football, I roamed the mountains and fields with my friends to relieve stress. In my school bag I had a frog that I had caught in a paddy field, and I planned to catch a snake later. Back then I felt like the entire world revolved around me.

But my ebullient self had to face its first ordeal. It happened after I had entered middle school when I sat my first test. I was playing football on the school field as usual one day when my form teacher called for me. I ran to the staffroom, not knowing why. My teacher was studying my report card and did not even glance up at me.

"Hyun-Soon Lee, did something happen to you recently?"
"Excuse me?"

My teacher held out my report card instead of answering.

"How could you have got these grades if nothing had happened?"

I studied my report card disbelievingly. The grades of the students in my class were listed in a column on the report card, according to their rankings. It was usually much quicker to search for my name from the top of the list. On that day, however, for some reason I couldn't find my name, even though I went far down the list. In the end, I could find my name only when I went all the way to the bottom of the score card. Fifty-fourth place. It was an unbelievable ranking. Fifty-fourth out of sixty students in my class! It was a ranking I had never received before, not since the day I was born.

"Are you in your right mind, or are you not? I thought you were hitting the books, but what is this? Pack your school bag quickly. I need to see your parents."

Bewildered, I brought my teacher to my house. I was indescribably befuddled. I couldn't comprehend how I could have got such grades. I was tremendously worried about what I should say to my parents, and how much scolding I'd receive.

"Hello. Mrs Lee, I'm Hyun-Soon's form teacher."

"Oh my, what a surprise."

My mother received my teacher with a look of surprise. And then she looked at me, who was coming in behind my teacher, her eyes asking the purpose of the teacher's visit. I simply hung my head down low.

"Mrs Lee, Hyun-Soon's grades have deteriorated considerably. How can a fellow who has come top of the class fall behind, not in fifth or tenth place, but in fifty-fourth place?"

As soon as my teacher sat down, she laid out my report card and started to admonish me. I wanted the ground to swallow me up. I couldn't even believe my grades myself, my mother must had been livid. However, after listening intently for some time to what my teacher was saying, my mother said, "Teacher, do not be overly worried. Hyun-Soon is a child who studies so diligently that he feels sad if he comes second. Perhaps there were some mistakes this time around."

My mother flashed me a warm smile as she usually did. Tears welled up in my eyes.

My mother had come to Seoul to study during the Japanese occupation, completed her middle and high school education, and then graduated from Gongju University's college of education. She understood the hearts of students more than anyone else did, because she had entered the teaching profession after graduating from college. She also cared for and cherished me more than anyone else did, because I had been neglected by my stern father as a second child. I was deeply sorry to disappoint a mother like her.

"Teacher, please let him off this time. He'll soon pull up his grades. Isn't that right, Hyun-Soon?"

In response to my mother's question I simply nodded, my eyes filled with tears. Then my teacher rose from her seat, perhaps because she had nothing more to say.

"I shall take your word for it then, Mrs Lee. Hyun-Soon, I'll let you off today because of what your mother has said, but you had better get your act together in future. Understood?"

That day I shut myself in my room and didn't even budge for several hours. Only then did I take a good look at myself. I was ashamed of my conceited behaviour, not knowing how high the sky was after I had received fairly good admission scores for middle school.

That was how I came to look at myself in the mirror for the first time after my first test in middle school. Until then, studying hadn't been so difficult. I could easily stay at the top of the class if I listened attentively to my teachers during class and carefully previewed and reviewed my work. I had presumed that this was possible because I had been born smart. Only now did I awaken to reality. The reality that the abilities of all students were comparable, and even if there were distinctions among them, they weren't that significant. That there was a very tiny difference between winning and losing. And that difference was determined by consistent hard work rather than innate intelligence.

Moreover, Seoul Middle School was populated by students who were as academically capable as the students at Gyeonggi Middle School. I might be left behind someday if I lowered my guard and relied only on my brains. Acquainted with this reality, I didn't want to injure my own pride again because of my grades. Therefore, from then on, I started studying seriously. I stopped playing football after school, and started going straight home after classes ended to revise my work. No longer did I play mischievous pranks during class, either. Back then there were no computers or televisions as there are now, and as a student I couldn't go into cinemas, so the truth was there was nothing I could do except study. Because I focused on my studies, I was able to restore my ranking to fourth place in the final exam.

Of course, since then I've never failed any exam. I have always achieved better-than-expected results for the important exams in my life, including my high school admission test, my university entrance exam, and all the tests I sat when studying overseas. In hindsight, coming in fifty-fourth place was the vaccination shot of my life. I was utterly shocked at the time, but I had the opportunity to look at myself carefully in the mirror because of experiencing an unthinkable setback. After that, I could always do my best without being conceited about it.

5

'What Will I Do?' Versus 'How Will I Live?'

There are people who are certain about what they want to do in life from an early age, but my career path wasn't so clear. I had only vaguely wondered if it would be nice to be a doctor or biologist. I'd been very fond of observing living things since I was young. I could never stay out of groups that collected insects, and I went around catching frogs and snakes. At school I always took biology classes as an extracurricular activity, and it was always a rewarding time when it came to dissecting rats and rabbits. Perhaps that was why I vaguely wanted to become a surgeon.

But when I told my form teacher that I wanted to attend medical school, he asked me to bring my father to him at once. This was a time when students with stellar grades would go to engineering school rather than medical school – just as outstanding students flock to medical school these days. My father had also graduated from engineering school. The meeting between my father and my form teacher concluded that I should, of course, attend engineering school. In a way, my career path changed on the advice of my parents and teacher.

When I share this story with others, they ask if I regret not going to medical school. Of course, I think that I could have put my abilities to use and become a fairly decent doctor if I had gone to medical school. But I've never once regretted majoring in engineering. My classes at engineering school comprised subjects that I enjoyed, and they were perfect for me.

I believe that there aren't many decisive moments in life when we have to decide something unequivocally. Life consists of the small decisions that we make each moment. Just as becoming a doctor was one of my prospects, becoming an engineer was also another prospect. The important thing was how hard I worked when I decided on one of my prospects.

Of course, it's very important to know what we like and what we excel in. But it's not desirable to decide on a career path too early, or to decide in an all-or-nothing manner. This is especially the case in engineering, where technology evolves rapidly with the times. It would be good to first determine the big picture, then carefully examine your prospects, which evolve with the times, and then explore professional fields that match your aptitudes.

Whether I went to medical school or engineering school, I wished to expand my abilities as much as I could. Therefore, once I had entered engineering school, I applied myself without hesitation to the study of engineering. I believe that anyone can achieve better-than-expected results if they place no limits on their own abilities and give their all in every decision they make.

6

In Everything, Foundation First

My life as an engineer began in earnest when I enrolled at the department of mechanical engineering at Seoul National University. At the department of mechanical engineering, I mainly learned how to create energy. Then, naturally, I grew interested in engines, which are one of the power sources that produce energy.

Engineering studies is difficult, then and now. In particular, as the maths at engineering school is exceedingly difficult, it's challenging to catch up with classes if you do not study hard. Throughout university, I conducted experiments every day, and lived buried in engineering textbooks. When I grew tired, I played tennis or went hiking with my friends. I still do that now, but I used to really love sports. Fuelled by youthful vigour, my friends and I would race up to Baegundae Peak on Mount Bukhan, or to the top of Mount Chiak – as though running a marathon – and competed against past records. University life could seem exhausting and dreary, but in those days I was filled with a passion to properly accomplish whatever I did.

However, if there's one thing I regret about my university days, it's that I studied engineering inefficiently. When I was solving differential equations or physics problems, there were no professors who could properly explain the meanings of the answers to those problems. Hence, though I always diligently solved the problems, I couldn't exactly comprehend what the results meant. Only after a long while did I understand that the answers to the problems I had so assiduously solved had been calculations of acceleration and referred to inertial force. Then my method of problem-solving changed, and I could come closer to the essence of the questions far more easily.

Therefore, even now, when I occasionally meet engineering professors, I implore them to teach students what the questions mean, and not simply to train them to solve problems. Nowadays, students don't have to solve problems directly, because they calculate using computers. But they need to know clearly what the answers mean, physically and mathematically. They can apply what they have learned to actual technological development only if they know the meanings of the answers they have obtained from their complex calculations.

During my university days, I also pondered how I could apply what I had learned from solving challenging and complex problems. I also wondered if I had solved them for nothing. But when I actually became an engineer and started to research engines seriously, I realised that the very foundation of my research was the knowledge I had gained as an engineering student. In whatever we do, only when we faithfully lay our foundation can we demonstrate our own abilities as much as we desire when we encounter something we really want to do later on.

7

South Korea Is Too Small for Me

I could study more deeply about engines after I enlisted in the military. As luck would have it, the Korea Air Force Academy announced that they were recruiting an instructor. The instructor who had taught about engines at the academy's engines lab had been discharged from the military, and the academy was recruiting a successor. I applied for the position without hesitation. And I was fortunately selected out of eleven applicants. I gained a golden opportunity to research aircraft engines. At the time, the academy's engines lab was furnished with dozens of aircraft engines. The lab possessed not just aircraft engines, but also the majority of the truck and jeep engines used by the military. The lab's facilities were as good as those in any university lab.

I spent four years in the engines lab disassembling and assembling aircraft propeller engines and jet engines. At the same time, I taught military cadets a range of subjects, including the operational principles of internal combustion engines and rocket engines, flight kinetics and propulsion engineering. The opportunity to research aircraft engines in the engines lab wasn't given to just anyone. I shut myself in the lab and researched, lectured, and absorbed knowledge about aircraft engines like a sponge. Soon I prided myself on being an aircraft engine expert.

But it was inevitable that I would become thirstier for knowledge the more I studied. When I read foreign research papers, which I obtained with much difficulty, I had to admit that South Korea's engine technology was still in its infancy. Having longed to amass the best skills, I gradually came to feel that South Korea was too small a country for me.

Can't I study engines more systematically? I wondered.

Back then it wasn't possible for just anyone to study abroad, as it is now. This was a time when the South Korean government selected and sent only six hundred people to study abroad every year. But that didn't dampen my eagerness to study abroad. With the dream to become the best in my field, I resolved to study abroad as soon as I was discharged from the Air Force Academy.

When I was searching for universities that excelled in the engine sector, the State University of New York in the United States caught my eye. Professor Irvine, an expert on rocket engines, was at that university. He had majored in electronic engineering in college and worked at Bell Labs, the world's best research institute, before starting to study again because he genuinely loved rockets. I wanted to research aircraft engines seriously under Professor Irvine.

At the time, there wasn't a single South Korean who had enrolled at and graduated from the mechanical engineering department of the State University of New York. It was a department that was difficult to graduate from. But I didn't care. I had to do everything for the first time myself, with no help from any college seniors, but I thought that nothing else mattered as long as I could research freely under an outstanding, world-famous professor. I submitted my application to the State University of New York after much difficulty, and waited for the results.

Part 2

Just Follow Your Heart

My dream of freely demonstrating my abilities as an engineer could be further enlarged because South Korea's automobile industry meshed well with the times, like a cogwheel.

8

Learn from the Best

When I was in the midst of preparing for overseas studies, a separate letter came together with a letter of admission from the State University of New York. The letter said that the semester hadn't started, but that it would be appreciated if I could arrive earlier at the college to assist with research. However, the person who had sent the letter wasn't Professor Irvine, by whom I wanted to be taught, but Professor O'Brien from the same department. I found it odd, but I hurriedly packed my bags and underwent the procedures for studying abroad. Since I had decided to study abroad, I thought it was better to go as soon as possible and adapt to the new environment.

As soon as I arrived in the United States and unpacked my bags at my place, I visited Professor O'Brien right away. He welcomed me warmly.

"Lee, it's great to see you. I'm sorry for asking you over here before the semester starts. I asked you because of an urgent project. I'd like you to start on this research with our assistant professor, starting from tomorrow."

"Starting from tomorrow?"

"Yes. There's a lot to do."

It turned out that Professor O'Brien had completed all the application procedures so that I could receive a scholarship, and had even prepared a research lab for me. I had no reason to hesitate any further. But Professor Irvine weighed on my mind.

"But…" I started to speak.

"Is there anything else you want to say?"

"Is Professor Irvine here?"

"Professor Irvine is now in Russia as a visiting professor. Why do you ask?"

"Ah, nothing. I'll do as you've instructed."

I said goodbye and left the research lab.

From the following day onwards, I joined Professor O'Brien's project and began the research work in earnest. Soon the semester started, and I was fully engrossed in the research. One day, Professor Irvine, who had returned from Russia, called for me. As soon as I entered his research lab, he promptly said, "Why are you working under Professor O'Brien?"

"Sorry?"

"You should be in my research team. I'm asking why you are there."

"I've been conducting research under Professor O'Brien since I arrived. He had already arranged a scholarship and a research lab for me."

"Is that so? Looks like there has been a mistake. Now that you know, stop going over there."

Several days later, there was a professors' meeting. When I entered the meeting room, five professors from the mechanical engineering department were seated, including Professor O'Brien and Professor Irvine. Looking at the situation, it seemed both professors had chosen me as their student before I came to the United States. Professor Irvine had entrusted my application to his secretary before leaving for Russia, and Professor O'Brien, not knowing what Professor Irvine had done, had taken me on as his own student. In short, there had been an administrative error. Professor Irvine, who came to know what had happened belatedly after returning from Russia, had convened the professors' meeting to rectify this situation.

After explaining the entire situation, Professor Irvine said to me: "I'm sorry, but this has happened, so you need to make a decision. Which professor do you want to research with? We'll respect your decision."

I was at a loss. I spoke honestly to the professors, who were waiting for a reply.

"It's difficult to decide on the spot. Could you give me some time to think it over?"

The meeting ended, and Professor Irvine called for me again.

"Who would have expected this to happen when I was in Russia? Please understand and come work with me."

As soon as I left Professor Irvine's research lab, Professor O'Brien called on me.

"I never knew that you wanted to study under Professor Irvine. I'm sorry for the mistake, but why don't you continue to research in our lab, since this has already happened? We've made considerable progress in the research, and if we stop here, won't it be a waste for you and me?"

Both professors had genuinely wanted me to work with them. I was thankful for that, but at the same time, it also put me in a tight spot. Of course, the professor I wanted to study under was Professor Irvine. As the chairman of the American Society of Mechanical Engineers, he was the most distinguished scholar in the engine sector. But I couldn't decide easily, because I had already been researching under Professor O'Brien for several months. If I decided to work under Professor Irvine, all the research I had conducted so far would go to waste.

After agonising over the matter for days, I finally came to a decision. I wanted to focus on quality. If my goal was to obtain a doctorate as soon as possible, it would be better to continue working under Professor O'Brien. But I wanted to be coached by the foremost authority in my field of study, even if it took more time. I had come all the way to the United States to acquire the best skills, so I believed that it was right to start again as I had originally intended.

I had reached a decision, but the truth was that Professor O'Brien weighed on my mind. We were working in the same department, so I would have to face him at least for another three to four years. I couldn't tiptoe around him whenever we met. After agonising over it, I visited Professor O'Brien.

"So, have you decided?"

"Yes, professor. I'm sorry, but I'd like to study under Professor Irvine."

Professor O'Brien looked obviously disappointed.

"Well, if that's what you want. I'll no longer hold you back."

Before he could finish speaking, I promptly told him my idea.

"But I shall finish the research I'm working on now before I leave. If I work on it for just a little longer, I might be able to obtain first-stage results. I'll work on it until then, then go to Professor Irvine."

For that reason, I could head over to Professor Irvine's research team only after I had worked on Professor O'Brien's research project for seven months. When I stepped into Professor Irvine's research lab, as I had wished to, he welcomed me warmly.

"Welcome. You've wasted your time through no fault of your own, hence I'll allow you to graduate if you publish just five papers in international journals under me. So do your best."

Professor Irvine patted my shoulder. My ears pricked up at what he said.

"Professor, really?"

It was a considerable privilege to speed up, even just a little, a combined masters and PhD programme that typically took more than five years to complete.

"Why would I lie to you? So, let's work well together."

And with that, I could start working in earnest on the research I had wanted to work on.

9

Getting an A Without Sitting the Test

Postgraduate classes were so intensive, they defied comparison with undergraduate classes. Moreover, not being proficient in English, I had considerable difficulty adapting to the classes. But no matter what, I was confident in my major. I was confident of not falling behind other students, because English wasn't so important on the courses for my major, and I had fully grasped the fundamentals when I was in South Korea.

One time, a professor was solving a differential equation. Postgraduate maths is so complex that an entire blackboard must be filled to solve one equation. That day too, the professor was engrossed in solving an equation that covered the whole blackboard. As I silently watched the professor solve the equation, I cautiously raised my hand.

"Professor, I can solve this differently."

The professor stared at me doubtfully.

"Really? Then come and try to solve this."

I stepped in front of the blackboard, with the other students behind me. As soon as I had solved the equation and turned around, the professor's eyes widened. In only seven lines I had solved the equation that had taken him thirty lines.

"Where did you learn this?" the professor asked, astonished.

"I didn't learn this from books, and I can often solve equations a little quicker because I solve them in this way."

The professor looked disbelieving at my reply. Then he hurriedly wiped the blackboard and gave me another equation. Of all differential equations, this was one with a very high level of difficulty.

"Then try to solve this too."

I could also solve this equation without difficulty. It took me more time than the first, but this time around I could figure out the answer using a far simpler method than the one the professor had used.

Then the professor marvelled at my solution.

"I can't believe that there was such a simple method. I'd absolutely no idea that this method existed, even though I've been teaching for decades."

The truth was I had accidentally discovered this method while I was teaching the cadets at the Korea Air Force Academy as an instructor. I had used textbooks originally published in foreign languages when I was teaching the military cadets, and after solving countless similar differential equations, at one point I realised I could solve these equations in a slightly simpler way. A simple method came to my mind, and when I applied the method, I could solve the equations far more easily, as I had expected.

The professor continued to marvel at my discovery and said, "Since I learned a great method from you today, it's all right even if you don't sit the test for this course. I'm giving you an A."

That was how I could receive an A for the course even without sitting the test.

10

I'll Teach *You*, Professor

I was in a hurry, having started later than the other students because I had been conducting research with Professor O'Brien. Fortunately, since my academic supervisor Professor Irvine had said he'd allow me to graduate if I published five papers, what I could do was to publish the papers as soon as possible. I couldn't graduate earlier than the other students, but at least I didn't want to graduate later than them. Time flew like an arrow as I researched conscientiously and published the findings in international journals. I published all five papers – after two and a half years. I was able to fulfil the number of papers much earlier than expected because I had devoted myself to research more assiduously, mindful that I had started later than the others. I ran to Professor Irvine, feeling relieved. He was sitting at his desk, reading the latest research.

"Professor, I've done it!"

He raised his eyes from the material he was reading and looked at me.

"What have you done?"

"As promised, I've published all five papers," I said expectantly.

Then he said, "All right, congratulations."

But that was all. I grew impatient.

"Professor, didn't you say last time that you'd let me graduate once I'd published five papers?"

Then Professor Irvine looked over his glasses and stared at me blankly. He looked like he had met a peculiar fellow. Exasperated, I reiterated, "I've published all five papers in international journals, as you said. So let me graduate as promised."

Professor Irvine then said, as if aghast, "Hey, do you know something? No one who has studied under me has graduated in five years. But now you're pestering me to let you graduate after two and a half years. Do you think this makes sense?"

"What do you mean? Professor, the other time you clearly…"

Before I could finish my sentence, he cut in.

"Did I? I've never said that."

The strength seemed to drain from my whole body. All this while, I had taken the professor at his word, shut myself in the research lab without resting for even a single day, conducted the research, and organised the findings. But the professor said that he had never promised any of that. I was so infuriated that I kicked the office door and walked away. I didn't want to speak any longer with a professor who failed to keep his promises. I left his research lab and walked around the campus for some time. It felt unfair that I had taken the professor at his word and spent more than two years running the race more diligently than the other students. I didn't want to see him again.

However, a month passed, and then a month and a half, and still Professor Irvine didn't call for me. If this continued, I wouldn't be able to graduate on time, much less graduate early. Tired of waiting, I visited his research lab again. As I was a mere foreign student, nothing good could come from locking horns with my academic supervisor.

"Professor, I'm here."

"Well. You've come."

The professor simply glanced at me briefly, and didn't even ask me to sit down. He looked like he was still upset. I thought I needed to negotiate with him.

"Professor, what exactly do you want?"

Then he pulled out a file, as if he had been waiting.

"Write this for your doctoral thesis. Then I'll let you graduate."

I studied the file carefully on the spot. It was a research project that measured the thermal changes in the boundary layer of aircraft turbine blades. It wasn't a bad idea for a research topic, but I wasn't pleased with it as a doctoral thesis topic. I closed the file.

"I can conduct research on this topic, as you wish. But…"

"But…?"

"I don't want to write my doctoral thesis on this topic."

"Why?"

"I have a topic I want to write about."

"What do you want to write about?"

"It's not difficult to measure temperature changes in the boundary layer of turbine blades, as you, professor, have proposed. I'd like to research the state of turbulence in the air layer that passes through turbines too."

"What?"

The professor stared at me for a while.

"That won't be a good idea."

"Why not?"

"I'm a boundary layer expert, not a turbulence expert. I know absolutely nothing about turbulence. I've never studied that."

That was true. But I didn't want to back down any further.

"Why not? If we can measure the boundary layer's temperature changes, we can also measure the state of turbulence in the entire turbine."

"Well, I guess so. But I'm not an expert on that, so I can't supervise you even if you do write a thesis on it."

"It doesn't matter. I'll conduct the research, and then I'll teach *you*, professor."

"What?"

The professor stared at me as if I were being absurd. Small wonder, because I had said I'd write my doctoral thesis on my own, without my professor's guidance, and I had even said that I'd teach him. But I looked back at the professor without yielding. I wanted to show him my resolve. Only after scowling at me for a long while did he ask me, with a serious look, 'This is a question that no one has solved so far. Can you really solve it?'

"Yes. I'll give it a try."

I replied with bravado, uncertain where my courage had come from.

"Ha, ha. I've lost. You really are an unstoppable fellow. Your ideas are good too, but this is the first time in my life that I've met an obstinate fellow like you. Know that you won't be graduating, and you'll gain nothing, if you fail in your experiments."

That was how I just barely obtained my professor's permission. The topic I had decided on required far more complex experiments and a lot more time to work on than the one my academic supervisor had proposed. There was also no thesis I could refer to, because no one had investigated that topic. Therefore, writing the thesis was several times harder. But I believed that there would be value in my doctoral thesis only if I wrote about a topic that no one else had addressed. Only then could I make a substantial impact in my field and have the merit of my research academically recognised. If I had studied abroad to simply obtain a doctorate, it would have been far easier to research the thesis topic that my academic supervisor had proposed. Then I could have received my supervisor's friendly guidance, written my thesis without effort, and graduated right away. But I wanted to research in an area that others had not and build up a true competence, even if I had to suffer. I wanted to write a thesis whose value could be recognised in academia, and to be recognised as an expert on aircraft engines. I was confident of fully withstanding the difficulties and hardships necessary to achieve these outcomes. As a result, the thesis I wrote became the very first to address this topic in the field. And because it was a topic that others hadn't addressed, I could successfully graduate earlier.

Even among young people of this generation, there are clearly people who excel at doing what they are told to do, but find it difficult to set their own goals and achieve them on their own initiative. These days it seems that we are sometimes exhausted even before we can discover what we want to do on our own, because there is already a fair amount of work that we must do and have been given to do. But there is a limitation on work that we are told to do. When difficulties or crises come our way, we will soon give up on such work. It is said that our brains get stressed about work that we are told to do, but enjoy work that is done voluntarily. Even difficult and demanding work.

In reality, we are unable to give up easily or make excuses about goals that we have decided on independently after mulling them over for days and nights. We somehow end up pushing ourselves to achieve these goals on our own. Me too. It was never an easy task to write a doctoral thesis on a topic that no one else had addressed. But I could give my utmost until its completion, because it wasn't something that anyone else had asked me to do: I did it because I personally felt the need to.

No doubt people who have no idea how hard I worked will look only at my specs and assess me. They will say that I could succeed because I was born in a good environment and with special talents. But that is because they know only one side of the story. I wasn't given much in my generation or in my environment. Unlike the present materially affluent generation, our generation was not at all affluent. Nothing was given to us for free, so we had to work hard and earn what we wanted. Ironically, I think that such an environment became good nourishment for my growth. I could constantly embrace challenges, because I didn't consider my inadequacies to be inevitable, and I had the will and passion to make up for them.

11

Standing at a Crossroads

I wanted to put my major to use and carry on with aircraft engine research after graduating from the State University of New York. But I soon found out that it wasn't easy to do so as a foreign student. This was because all the funds pertaining to aircraft engine research were doled out by the United States Department of Defence at that time. There was no way the Department of Defence was going to entrust such an important project to a mere foreign student. I was disappointed, but I turned my career path towards automobile engines. That became the best decision and opportunity for me.

The 1980s was a period when the automobile industry in the United States was at its peak of growth. Global automobile companies had lined up in Detroit, Michigan. I joined one of them – GM. GM was the world's most prestigious automobile company, with more than one thousand two hundred postdoctoral researchers like me. Therefore, when it came to engine research, the company freely supported any employee. I could freely research the newest engines in my own personal research lab that the company provided, with no lack for anything.

While I was absorbed in researching the newest engine models at GM, Hyundai was just starting to manufacture automobiles under its own brand in South Korea and export them overseas. In 1976, Hyundai Motors had started to mass-produce South Korea's very first unique car model. Subsequently, it launched car models like the Hyundai Pony and Hyundai Stellar, and began to establish itself in the domestic market. Hyundai Motors was planning to continue its successful streak by exporting the Hyundai Excel to the US market. That Hyundai Motors could export automobiles to the US market, which was well known for its fastidious regulations, was a remarkable thing worth taking pride in.

However, technically speaking, the Hyundai Pony and Hyundai Excel didn't represent the technical skills of Hyundai Motors. That was because the company had bought the drawings of key components – such as the engines, said to be the heart of an automobile, and the gearboxes –from overseas to manufacture them; it had independently designed and built only the car bodies. Hyundai Motors was producing around a hundred thousand such cars per year. The company wasn't satisfied, and was thinking of further expanding its domestic automobile business. The company also had plans to construct large-scale factories that could manufacture three hundred thousand cars yearly from 1978 onwards. But the domestic politics of the time thwarted its plans. There were changes in South Korea's economic policies as the country's political situation underwent rapid change. Back then, the government officials who made the policies were sceptical about developing South Korea's automobile industry.

"If we want to develop our economy, shouldn't we develop industries in which we are more competitive, or that are more advantageous for us compared with foreign products? It's better to leave aside industries that are not."

In other words, government officials thought that it was better to further promote industries that were already competitive at the time, like the textile industry, and to give up on industries like the automobile industry, which lacked technology and were hardly competitive. This came as a bolt from the blue for Hyundai Motors, which was just about to expand its automobile business. If these policies came to pass, all the efforts devoted to its automobile business in the past ten years would go down the drain.

Hyundai Motors met with government officials and strove to explain until the company was blue in the face, and to help the officials understand why it was both important and possible to develop the automobile industry. But these efforts did not suffice. On the contrary, the government pressured Ju-Yung Chung, then head of the Hyundai Group, to choose between heavy industry and the automobile industry. Chairman Chung decided on the automobile industry, after much consideration. The reason was that the company could build the facilities for and invest in heavy industry again in the future, but it might be left behind and unable to catch up later if it didn't develop its automobile business right now.

As the situation unfolded, Chairman Chung placed the survival of the company on the line and decided to develop the automobile business. That being the case, what should the company start doing first? After serious deliberation, Chairman Chung said: "It has been more than ten years since our company started manufacturing automobiles. We can't not have our own engines. From now on, we shall build engines using our very own technology."

Chairman Chung believed that Hyundai Motors had to prioritise technological independence if it was to develop its automobile business. However, there were considerable objections from within the company. There were many who thought it would be impossible to create engines on our own. Even engineers balked at the idea.

"Please think what will happen if Mitsubishi hear that Hyundai is developing engines independently. They will no longer help us. They won't transfer their engine technology to us, and our car production will suffer a setback right away. We mustn't even start developing our own engines if we aren't confident of resolving this problem properly."

Back then, Hyundai Motors was paying high prices to import engine technology from the Japanese company Mitsubishi. Therefore, if Hyundai were to develop its own engines, Mitsubishi would be the most affected. But Chairman Chung was adamant.

"For how long will our so-called automobile company import and use engines built by other companies? An engine is like the heart of a car. We can no longer delay the development of our own engines."

Consequently, in early 1983, Hyundai Motors finalised plans to build a research institute for engine development. In September 1983, the New Engine Development Plan was implemented by the company. Now, with the plan under way, the company could no longer delay developing its own engines. The executives of Hyundai Motors hurriedly set out in search of talented individuals who could participate in engine development.

12

Nothing Is Impossible

If Hyundai Motors wanted to develop its own engines, above all it needed talented people who could develop engines. However, in those days, people who had such skills were practically non-existent in South Korea. For that reason, the executives of Hyundai Motors were keeping their eye on people who had previously gone abroad. Whenever they visited the United States, they visited Detroit and met with South Koreans who were studying in schools and research institutes or working at automobile companies. Hence, on several occasions, I had attended gatherings to which Hyundai Motors had invited me.

In the summer of 1983, I was spending my holiday in South Korea. Hyundai Motors suddenly called to say they wanted to meet me. My older brother had a friend who worked at the American automobile company Ford, and it looked as if he had recommended me to Hyeon-Dong Shin, an adviser who was heading the New Engine Development Plan at Hyundai Motors.

I visited Hyundai's headquarters. There I met President Se-Yung Chung of Hyundai Motors – with whom I was already acquainted, because he had visited the United States every year for the Detroit road show and had offered me words of encouragement every time.

As soon as he saw me, he said, "Dr Lee, I'm really pleased to see you again in South Korea. We're planning to develop our own engines this time around, and we're very much in need of talented people like you. Why don't you take this opportunity to work with us?"

I appreciated the offer, but I respectfully turned him down and returned to the United States, because I had absolutely no intention of working at Hyundai at the time. But Hyundai didn't give up easily on recruiting people. Every day, I received calls from the secretarial offices of Chairman Ju-Yung Chung and President Se-Yung Chung. They constantly tried to persuade me to work with them to develop South Korea's automobile industry.

I began to feel troubled as they repeated their offer. At GM I could freely conduct the research that I wanted to do. This wasn't a decision that I could make easily – to leave such a wonderful environment and move to Hyundai Motors, which was no different from a wasteland.

In those days, Hyundai Motors was a second mover that had just began exporting automobiles. The company had started out a good hundred years later than automobile companies in developed countries. It was unthinkable that such a company could compete against large automobile companies like GM and survive. But there was something inexplicable that kept making me hesitate to turn them down.

My family quietly welcomed Hyundai's recruitment offer. It seems that my father, who had sent all three of his sons to study abroad, wanted me – his second son – to return to South Korea on this opportunity. My wife, who had given birth to our first child and struggled to adapt to life in dreary Detroit, was also hoping to return to South Korea. But I couldn't actually decide with ease.

Should I stay in my stable job at a global automobile company, or should I move to Hyundai and take on new challenges?

My dilemma deepened day by day. Whatever decision I made, it was clear that my decision would become a turning point in my life. Perhaps back then I tried to foresee my life as far ahead as possible and to assess the magnitude of my dreams. Then after questioning myself for six months about what I really wanted, I felt my heart leaning towards one company.

All right, let's do this. It's clearly not an easy task to develop engines at Hyundai. But since it's something no one has done before, shouldn't I take it up? It's a foolhardy challenge, but isn't nothing impossible?

Above all, I wanted to attempt building distinctive engines on my own. Though I had to start laboriously in an automobile wasteland, it would be more rewarding and valuable than anything else if I succeeded.

Back then, I reckoned that it would be more rewarding to offer support, however meagre, to South Korea's nascent automobile industry than to spend my entire life as a researcher at a global automobile company. My dream of freely demonstrating my abilities as an engineer could be further enlarged because South Korea's automobile industry meshed well with the times, like a cogwheel.

From the moment I made up my mind, there was nothing much I feared. Right away, I told GM that I wanted to resign. Then my superior tried to dissuade me.

"Look here, Dr Lee. South Korea is a backward country that has been lagging behind in the automobile industry for some time.

Do you want to squander your talents there? Don't do that, stay here. If you stay, I'll see to it that you receive the best treatment."

Employee welfare and treatment were stable at GM because it was a gargantuan company with seven hundred and sixty thousand employees at the time. Even without this offer from my superior, I was already enjoying a very affluent lifestyle at the company. But my heart was already leaning towards South Korea.

"Still, I want to give it a try."

Then my superior looked disappointed, as though it had been inevitable.

"It can't be helped, if that's what you want. But it's not going to be easy. You've no idea because you're young now, but the automobile industry is not a field where second-mover companies like Hyundai can catch up easily."

My superior was genuinely concerned for me.

"I'll make you an offer. If you go to Hyundai and find it unbearable, you can always come back again. I'll keep your research lab vacant until then."

I thanked my superior for his kindness, and left GM. And right away, I packed my bags and boarded a plane bound for South Korea. Nothing had been decided about the conditions under which I'd be working or what treatment I'd receive at Hyundai. But I decided not to dither any longer. The best challenge of my life had already begun.

13

That Guy Is a Con Artist

In April 1984, when spring flowers filled the streets, I arrived at Gimpo Airport. On my first day at work, I met with Chairman Ju-Yung Chung.

"Dr Lee, thank you for joining us. Please work hard for our company from now on. I'll freely provide whatever you want."

However, when I joined the company, there was literally nothing there. Unlike GM, which had a line-up of twenty-five thousand researchers, Hyundai had no researchers and no research institute, and even the land for building the research institute wasn't ready. All Chairman Chung did was simply introduce five subordinates to me.

"Take these people and start developing an engine quickly."

"Excuse me? With only these five people?"

"Ha, ha. In return I'll provide whatever you need, so just let me know," Chairman Chung said with a hearty laugh. I wasn't certain if he knew how I felt.

After our meeting, I left the chairman's office looking dumbfounded. I went to my office and organised my things, and thought intently about what had to be done hereafter. Then a man abruptly stepped into my office.

"Are you Hyun-Soon Lee?"

"Yes, but…"

"I'm your superior."

"Is that so? I haven't had the chance to greet you. I'm Hyun-Soon Lee."

When I introduced myself, he let his discomfort show, as if he had no intention to be greeted.

"I think you made a mistake coming here."

"A mistake? What do you mean?"

"I'm talking about the engine that you're developing, it's not going to work. What exactly were you plotting when you came here?"

His eyes were filled with suspicion and mistrust.

"Plotting?"

I felt aversion towards my superior, who was accusing me on our first meeting.

"I'm asking if you haven't come to con the company. I've no idea what sweet talk you beguiled the chairman with, but you can't fool me."

By then, I could no longer hold back.

"Why exactly do you conclude that I'm a con artist?"

"Must I really say it? How can a young and inexperienced person develop an engine? Do you think that engine development is child's play? Even if you want to con other people, you should do it within limits. Tsk, tsk."

"You're going too far with your words. I haven't even started with engine development. If I fail later, let's talk then."

I retorted without yielding. Our gazes collided in the air. Tension hung between us. Then my superior looked away displeased and said, "You don't get what I said."

He walked out of the room without looking back. Left alone in the office, I strove to repress my anger. I hadn't expected rousing cheers. Nor had I thought that life at Hyundai would be easy. But I had never imagined being treated so harshly to my face. From then on, a war started between my superior and me. My superior denigrated me whenever he had the opportunity.

"That guy is conning the company. Don't be fooled by him."

And he interfered with everything I did, as if to prove that I was conning the company. Whenever I went to him to obtain approval, he invariably hurled the files at me. There were also occasions when I stood for several hours while he denigrated me. When I was out of the office on business trips, he even picked on my subordinates.

Once, I was in a board meeting with President Se-Yung Chung. The topic of engines came up in the middle of the meeting, and my superior said abruptly, "New technologies and new engines sound good, but we can't develop them. How can we create engines that even Mitsubishi finds difficult to make? Live or die, we must use Mitsubishi's technology."

Someone who held the title of director of research and development at Hyundai Motors had contended that technological independence was completely impossible, and that we had to use Mitsubishi's technology. After listening silently, I was so frustrated that I asked him, "Director, so when do you think we can be technologically independent?"

He retorted at once, "Good question! President, I'm not saying that we shouldn't be technologically independent. We must. But how can it be as easy as it sounds? This is what I think. It's impossible for us to become independent in engine technology right now, given our current standards. Let's first become independent in the chassis technology that's used to support car bodies by the year 2000, and then develop our own engines."

I asked again, "So when do you suggest we develop our own engines?"

"I think it has to be around 2010."

"2010? Isn't that twenty-six years away? By then you, director, and I will no longer be around, so when the time comes, how will the company develop engines?"

The director seemed to be acknowledging that we could never develop our own engines by ourselves. When I pressed him again, he seemed about to lose his cool.

"Dr Lee, I'm speaking realistically, instead of pouring enormous sums of money into developing new engines which are terrible, like you are. President, if the engines Dr Lee designs work, pigs will fly."

I didn't back down.

"Perhaps that might happen."

As our intense war of nerves persisted, President Chung, who couldn't watch on, intervened.

"Why do the two of you argue whenever you meet? It's frustrating that the engines may or may not be developed even if the two of you join forces."

Neither of us budged an inch, however.

Looking back, the conflict between my superior and me wasn't simply a psychological war between two people. Our conflict resembled a wall that perfectly represented our current state of technological standards. In those days, almost no one at Hyundai believed that we could develop our own engines by ourselves.

Therefore, the company's board of directors was very worried that the fact that we were developing our own engines might upset Mitsubishi. They were needlessly afraid that their carefully maintained relationship with Mitsubishi might fall apart because they coveted technological independence.

But my mind was occupied with only one goal. It was my ambition, as an engineer, to develop our own engines by our own strength. If I were to be pushed aside by forces that supported Mitsubishi, the plans to develop engines would be shelved before we could even start.

There's nothing I'll be able to do if I'm pushed out by them. I must become stronger if I want to survive here.

I was more determined than ever.

But I still had a long way to go.

14

Dr Lee, What Did You Come Here to Do?

The first thing I did after joining Hyundai Motors was to look into plots of land suitable for building the research institute. I had to start everything from scratch. Back then, several locations deemed suitable for building the research institute had been shortlisted, but we hit a rough patch because most could not be issued with construction permits. After visiting several locations, I reported to Chairman Ju-Yung Chung that there was a twenty thousand *pyeong* plot of land in Sosa district, Bucheon.[3]

He said, "Isn't twenty thousand *pyeong* a little small for building a research institute? We have a piece of land in Mabuk, so let's build it there."

This plot of land, in the village of Mabuk in Yongin County, Gyeonggi Province, had been bought by Chairman Chung when Hyundai was building the Gyeongbu Expressway. He readily offered the land – which Hyundai hadn't used for more than ten years, even when the company was at the peak of its expansion – to build the research institute. It was a key moment when I could

---

3 One *pyeong* is equivalent to 3.3 square metres. This plot of land was approximately sixty-six thousand square metres.

guess how devoted Chairman Chung was to developing our own engines.

As soon as the land had been provided and the construction of the research institute started, I visited the site day after day. Chairman Chung did too. Every weekend he wore sneakers to the construction site and took command. One day, he looked blankly at the rising building and said, "Dr Lee, build a five-storey research institute, and add an underground area as well as a lift."

We had planned to build a three-storey research institute.

"Chairman, won't the research institute be too large for its occupants?"

I tried to talk him out of it, but he paid no heed.

"Proceed with that for now, even if there's a limit to making space for it."

That was how the research institute became a five-storey building. The construction of the research institute was completed speedily because the entire Hyundai Group worked together during the construction. In the early days after construction was completed, the building was colossal, so we lent the fourth and fifth storeys to Hyundai Precision & Industries Corporation (now Hyundai Mobis). But as the number of people at the research institute gradually grew and our facilities expanded, we subsequently had to expand the building to more than twice its original size.

When the construction of the research institute was in full swing, I was also busy recruiting research staff. The research institute, which had started with only five researchers when I first joined the company, recruited ninety-eight new employees six months later, and established the foundation of a respectable research institute.

When I was recruiting the research staff, I deliberately focused on recruiting entry-level rather than experienced candidates. The reason was that in those days no one in South Korea had developed an engine, and the engines we planned to develop were considerably different from the existing ones. I decided that entry-level employees, who could conduct research while learning everything new from the outset, would be better than experienced candidates who had a superficial knowledge of engines. Therefore, at one point the average age of the research staff at the institute was only around thirty-one years old. Having assembled young, ambitious, talented people, we could carry out engine development in a free and creative environment.

As the research institute gradually livened up, I heard from Hyundai's planning office. They suggested that we should visit the Ministry of Trade and Industry (now the Ministry of Trade, Industry and Energy) now that we had started engine development work.

Together with employees from the planning office, I met with the director of the mechanical industry bureau at the Ministry of Trade and Industry. After he learned of my background and work experience, the director promptly said, "Dr Lee, haven't you got this wrong?"

"What have I got wrong?"

"There isn't any work for a doctorate holder in an automobile company, is there? You should be a professor at a university if you're a doctorate holder, what did you come here to do?"

I couldn't speak, because it was absurd.

"There are more than one thousand two hundred doctorate holders at GM."

"Because that's GM. We can simply pay for technical designs and manufacture accordingly, so is there any work for you like you did at GM?"

There was nothing more I could say. That was all a high-ranking civil servant in our country knew about the automobile industry at this time. No doubt most people would have thought the same, because no one in South Korea's automobile industry had a doctorate in those days. In that social environment, Hyundai Motors had little choice but to push on and move forwards with the task of developing our own engines, alone.

Part 3

Starting Work in a Technology Wasteland

People who have clear goals can't give up easily. They have no choice but to hold out silently until their situation changes. That doesn't mean that they thoughtlessly stop work and wait. They must continually exert themselves until they find a breakthrough.

15

The Best Begin with Their Sights Set on the Future

Even amid the twists and turns, Hyundai Motors's New Engine Development Plan was getting under way, one step at a time. On 15 November 1984, the Mabuk Research Institute was finally unveiled in the village of Mabuk, Geumseong Township, Yongin County, Gyeonggi Province. It was barely six months after engineering construction had begun.

As soon as the researchers moved in, one after the other, the Mabuk Research Institute started to operate so busily we couldn't tell day from night. We installed all sorts of experimental equipment needed for engine development, and we carried out engine development projects at the same time as we trained the new recruits. Only then could I too devote myself fully and seriously to research.

After the research institute took shape, the very first thing we did was to decide what kind of engine to develop. Initially, everything was bleak. Nothing had been decided about the specifications of the engine we were going to develop, or about which types of automobiles to fit with the newly developed engine. And it was my job to straighten these questions out. After agonising over them, I fully revised the plan to push ahead with an existing engine model, and announced that we were going to develop an engine with the newest specifications. I christened it the 'Alpha engine'. This was how the so-called Alpha engine project started. But voices of dissent broke out all over.

"Are you going to develop the newest engine? An engine that even Mitsubishi couldn't develop yet? Are you in your right mind?"

Everyone in the company responded with disbelief. Hyundai's Ulsan Research Institute objected especially strongly. At the time, there was a team in Ulsan that imported Mitsubishi's technology to manufacture engines. They criticised the plan to abandon the existing engine manufacturing methods and create our own engines as foolhardy. They stressed that even if we created our own engines, we would have to develop an old-style engine that had a high chance of success, rather than a new model that would have a high failure rate.

Hyundai's engineers had good reason for objecting so vigorously. They had previously developed an engine independently and failed. It had been a project to remodel the Hyundai Pony's gasoline engine into a diesel engine in 1980. Back then, the engine development team had obtained help from a German service company to create a trial engine, and had even completed a trial out on the Autobahn. But they hit a deadlock as development work continued, and the project was called off for various reasons. Eventually, the diesel engine project became an experience of failure for the engineers.

In that context, it was hard for them to believe a young researcher who said out of the blue that he was going to create the newest electronic fuel-injection multivalve engine, which no one had heard of or seen before. They told me that engine development work didn't consist solely of a poorly devised plan and the desire to implement it. But I had other ideas. I didn't believe that creating an engine by our own strength was impossible, and I thought that creating an old-style engine wouldn't suit market conditions – and as an engineer, I also thought it would be meaningless.

"We can't settle for the status quo forever. I don't know how long it'll take to develop our own engine, but the technological gap between us and more advanced companies will only widen if we create an uncompetitive old-style engine. What's the point in doing that? I want to create an engine that is competitive on the market, at the end of the day."

Of course, my goal was somewhat foolhardy. Back then it was difficult to find the engine specifications we were after in South Korea. It was a form of technology that hadn't yet been commercialised overseas. It was no doubt difficult for the engineers to comprehend, because a company that had just planned to create an engine on its own was leaping straight over the intermediate phase to produce the world's best engine right away.

But I didn't think that it was impossible to create the latest engine on our own. I thought this not because I had a rash and reckless working style. I simply knew for a fact that it was entirely possible to actualise the engine I wanted to create.

The truth was that the Alpha engine was exceptional in performance. GM was already developing an engine with similar specifications at the time. That was why Hyundai could compete adequately against overseas companies only if we developed an engine with the newest specifications. I knew this, and it was one more reason why I couldn't abandon this plan. Ultimately, the only thing that remained was to push ahead unwaveringly with my idea.

"If we set our sights on engine models that other companies have already developed because we started out late, we will never catch up with the leading companies. Even though it'll be a little difficult in the early phase, won't we achieve the highest standards of technology in a short time span and become competitive only if we set our sights on the newest models?"

This was how I motivated the engineers at the research institute. Of course, not every member of Hyundai agreed with me, but at least the engineers at the Mabuk Research Institute believed in me and followed my lead. I'm so thankful when I think about that now.

16

Foes or Allies?

Most people aren't happy about attempting something new. Even when it brings about positive changes. Therefore, it's inevitable that people who attempt something new will always come up against the objections of those who adhere to existing ways of doing things.

When I joined Hyundai Motors, the company drew by hand, on drawing boards, when designing its vehicles. There was a need to introduce a new method as soon as possible to raise the company's technical skills to world standards. I instructed the draughtsmen to abandon existing methods and work using computers from then on. The draughtsmen objected vehemently.

Not that I couldn't understand their reaction. It would have been difficult for them to change overnight the way they worked, which they had been accustomed to for all this time, and they'd have been terrified of losing their jobs if they made the slightest mistake. But a system change was inevitable if the company wanted to keep up with advanced technologies. Hence, I started to persuade them.

"To raise our technological standards, we've little choice but to introduce an advanced system. I don't plan to dismiss you all.

The company will retrain everyone, so don't worry, and please work with me."

To allay their fears of change, I also didn't forget to promise them that I'd certainly offer them full institutional support. Only then did the draughtsmen believe and join me.

But the constraints and pressures from some executives who had inadequate understandings of technology worsened with each passing day. They openly claimed that my plan would never succeed. There were even people who accused me of being a con artist. I was preoccupied with research, but I didn't feel at ease because of these criticisms. That said, I couldn't go to every single one of them and persuade them. I had no choice but to focus silently on my work.

One day, I was conducting research in the research lab. I heard that Chairman Ju-Yung Chung wanted to see me urgently. I stopped the experiment and rushed hurriedly from the Mabuk Research Institute in Yongin to Hyundai Group's headquarters in Seoul's Gye-dong district. As soon as I entered the chairman's office, Chairman Chung met me with a grim face.

"Dr Lee, can the project you're working on really succeed?"

Without even knowing why he had asked, I answered frankly, "Yes, chairman. Aren't we working on it because it can succeed?"

Then Chairman Chung looked at me with a fuming expression.

"Don't even think of giving me a false report. I'll ask again. Can it really succeed?"

He looked me straight in the eye. I felt his resolve to never tolerate any lies. I stood still, not knowing why he had asked. I couldn't explain the prospects of engine development in a word or two. Then he placed a document in front of me. On the document was written:

"The new electronic fuel-injection engine technology that your company has inquired about has a high level of technical difficulty, hence it is difficult to mass-produce and has absolutely no economic viability. As a future technology that has been tested in school research labs, it is not suitable for research in automobile companies. Therefore, we have absolutely no plans to commercialise this technology."

I closed the document.

"What's this?"

"Can't you tell? It's Mitsubishi's response."

As Chairman Chung had said, it was a written response to our inquiry as to whether it was indeed possible to develop the engine we intended to develop, and if so, whether Mitsubishi had any plans to develop it. It looked as if the representative of the Ulsan Research Institute, who was doubtful about the Alpha engine project, had consulted Mitsubishi. Chairman Chung had read the written response and misunderstood that I was developing an engine that had no possibility of being brought to fruition.

"There has been much talk in the company about how the Alpha engine can't work. Try to explain that."

Chairman Chung was now pressing me for an answer. Exasperated, I let out a sigh. Mitsubishi could maintain an amicable relationship with us because they transferred their technology to us and collected royalties from us. They wanted us to continue to import and use their outdated technology. Of course, they couldn't possibly be pleased that we were developing our own engine.

"Chairman Chung, let me ask you just one question. Is Mitsubishi our ally or our foe?"

Then Chairman Chung said, as if it were a given, "Our foe, of course."

"But why do you believe what the foe says?"

Chairman Chung then stared at me blankly, speechless. I had nothing more to add either.

It was later revealed that Mitsubishi knew better than anyone else of the Alpha engine's superiority. Therefore, even at the time when they sent us the written response, they were already developing an engine that had specifications similar to the Alpha engine. Meanwhile, they sent us such an absurd written response to hold us back. However, back then, I couldn't thoroughly explain to Chairman Chung, who wasn't an expert on engines, the prospects of bringing the Alpha engine to fruition. In the end, this was all I said before I left his office: "I shall get going if you've nothing more to add. I came hurriedly in the middle of experiment, so I'd better pick up where I left off."

Then from behind me came Chairman Jung's voice: "Dr Lee, go quickly and conduct your experiment. You must succeed."

17

Should I Just Give Up?

In those days, Hyundai Motors imported from Mitsubishi every core technology used in automobiles, such as engine and gearbox technology. If Mitsubishi were to decide not to sell the technology used to produce engines and gearboxes, Hyundai would inevitably be unable to manufacture automobiles. Therefore, there were Hyundai Motors executives who would do anything for Mitsubishi.

Chairman Ju-Yung Chung had seen through this earlier. He knew that it was of paramount importance that we should possess core technology. For that reason, he was more deeply devoted than anyone else to developing our own engines. If we failed to develop our own engines, we would have little choice but to depend on other companies like Mitsubishi that possessed their own original technology. Consequently, developing our own engines was a project upon which Hyundai Motors's survival depended. I had to lead the project to success, no matter what.

One day, after coming back from a business trip to Germany to buy needed auto parts, I found my office empty. My secretary was gone, and my desk was nowhere to be seen. It was too preposterous, so I asked the head of administration, "What happened?"

"Didn't you know? You've been dismissed from your post," he said calmly.

Being dismissed from my post meant that I could stay in the company, but I had to completely step back from what I had been handling so far. What he said implied that there was nothing I could do for the Alpha engine project, which had just begun. Overnight, I had been ousted from my post as head of new engine development and become a powerless technical adviser.

My desk was placed starkly in a corridor next to an emergency exit. I was reduced to spending my time at a single iron desk in a corridor with people passing by, without a personal office.

Chairman Chung was swamped with the setting up of Hyundai Electronics. Therefore, he had absolutely no idea that I had been dismissed from my post. But I couldn't go to Chairman Chung directly and launch a complaint. I had no choice but to sit in the corridor and spend my time there. The more I thought about it, the more dumbstruck I was, but there was no other way around it.

My dismissal had been caused by pressure from Mitsubishi. Back then, there were numerous Hyundai Motors executives who were very close to Mitsubishi. Moreover, as the major shareholder of Hyundai Motors, Mitsubishi wielded significant influence. With the intention of obstructing Hyundai's development of its own engines, Mitsubishi had twisted the arms of executives with whom they were acquainted into dismissing me from my post.

My superior, who had misgivings about me, suspended me from all the projects that I had been involved in, as if he had been waiting for that moment. And he deployed all of my subordinates, who had been developing the Alpha engine, to remodel the Mitsubishi Orion engine. It had already been agreed that the

Orion engine would be used between Mitsubishi and Hyundai after being jointly developed by both companies. The Alpha engine project was in danger of disintegrating into thin air. I was hurt and frustrated, because we had no time to lose on developing our engine. Ousted into a corner of the corridor, without power or position, I felt exceptionally forlorn.

Should I just give up?

There were days when this thought crossed my mind as I sat in a corner of the corridor. I wanted to resign right away because I felt aggrieved and angry. Even now, the research lab where I had been working at GM was still vacant and waiting for me. I wanted to resign and return to the United States at once. But I steeled myself.

Who would be the most pleased if I gave up here and returned to the United States? Wouldn't it be Mitsubishi and its followers, who accused me of being a con artist? My pride won't allow me to back down as they wish. I don't want to live the rest of my life vilified as a con artist. I must hold out here, no matter what.

I resolved to grit my teeth and hold out. I was upset and aggrieved, but on the other hand I wasn't going to just back down, because of my pride.

When we work towards our dreams, there are times when ordeals come our way, and it's as if we find ourselves trapped in a tunnel with the front and back exits firmly blocked. It seems as though the situation will continue forever, and our frustration further deepens when we feel that we can't change the situation at all on our own. Avoiding or giving up on the situation may seem like a better solution.

But people who have clear goals can't give up easily. This is because they can't proceed to the next step without going through this process. When that happens, they have no choice but to hold out silently until their situation changes. That doesn't mean that they thoughtlessly stop work and wait. They must continually exert themselves until they find a breakthrough.

Furthermore, I couldn't take it lying down. Having lost all my power overnight, I had nothing to do even if I went to work. I decided to prepare myself so that I could start developing engines right away when the time came for me to do it again someday. I read research papers published abroad, and closely analysed rival companies' data. Whenever other employees passed by, my ears burned, but I decided not to let what others said bother me. The only thing I could trust was my own competence.

Time passed. I slowly became an invisible man in the research institute. I could put up with reading research papers alone all day long. But lunchtime was a chore. Even when I had to queue for a seat because there were no seats in the company cafeteria, no one sat next to me. People didn't want to be penalised for being close to me. I was upset and furious. But whenever that happened, I resolved to hold back my resentment.

I will definitely get back at the Mitsubishi scoundrels who tried to obstruct Hyundai's technological independence.

Before I knew it, six months had passed. The number of research papers I had read in that period exceeded a thousand. Then my situation quickly changed, as if everything had been a lie. An order was issued to reinstate me as head of engine development. Chairman Ju-Yung Chung, who was done with setting up Hyundai Electronics, had heard about my plight and taken action at once.

The reinstatement order came at an unexpected moment, without any forewarning. I felt as if I had encountered the sun after rising continually in a sky filled with dark clouds. As soon as I was reinstated, I dived straight into engine development. I was already prepared, because I had been constantly reading research papers and getting myself ready while I was away from the project. Now I had no time to lose.

18

Mitsubishi Offers to Reduce Its Royalties by Half

Mitsubishi made considerable efforts to stop Hyundai Motors developing its own engines. At every opportunity, Mitsubishi would openly say: "Hyundai say they are developing their own engines, but they will design engines that Mitsubishi created thirty years ago. We've no idea why they are doing that when it's futile to spend money on engine development. It's better not to start in the first place."

Even when I heard remarks like these, I simply did what I needed to do, silently.

One day, while I was experimenting on an engine, Chairman Ju-Yung Chung visited me.

"Dr Lee, are you busy?"

"Chairman, what's the matter?"

"If it's all right, let's have dinner together."

Chairman Chung looked like he was in a very good mood that day.

"So, is the engine development coming along well?"

"Yes, it's going as planned, but…"

I was curious about what Chairman Chung wanted to say. As if he could read my mind, he said, "Chairman Kubo came by today."

"Is Chairman Kubo the chairman of Mitsubishi?"

Chairman Tomio Kubo was a prominent figure in Japan who was treated as the 'god of engineers'. He had become famous after designing the engine for the Zero fighter aircraft at the age of twenty-eight during the Second World War. Chairman Chung and Chairman Kubo were such close friends that it was rumoured that Chairman Kubo had lent ship designs to Chairman Chung when Hyundai began its shipbuilding business.

"I didn't tell you, but Chairman Kubo visited me last year too. Can you guess why?"

Not that I didn't have any idea. But I waited quietly for Chairman Chung to continue.

"Chairman Kubo said: 'Designing engines isn't an easy task. The young man who came to Hyundai is going to design engines because he studied in the United States and worked for GM. But building engines isn't possible with just one doctorate holder.'"

I simply listened without saying a word.

Chairman Chung continued, "But this time around, he said: 'Mitsubishi will assist with everything Hyundai needs, so why take the risk to make engines?' He's worried that it'll be a waste of time and money."

"Really?" I said calmly.

I didn't find that surprising, because this was the company that had got me dismissed from my post in order to stop Hyundai developing its own engines.

"And do you know what he said? He'll cut our engine royalties by half right away if we stop developing our own engines now. Dr Lee, did you hear me? Half of the royalties, half."

Chairman Chung leaned back with a guffaw, as if that was good news. But my face hardened. Half of the royalties was a colossal sum. In 1988, the year of the Summer Olympics in South Korea, South Korea experienced the 'my car' boom, when Hyundai Motors made such tremendous profits that it didn't have enough cars to sell – but half the year's net profits were still paid to Mitsubishi as royalties.[4] It would be of immense benefit to Hyundai if Mitsubishi were to reduce the amount by half. It was an amount that even Chairman Chung couldn't disregard.

"So, what did you say?"

"What do you think? Of course, I said no," Chairman Chung said with a laugh.

However important it was to develop our own engines, it wasn't easy to flatly refuse Chairman Kubo's offer.

Quietly, I asked Chairman Chung, "Chairman, it would be of tremendous benefit for the company if the royalties were reduced by half, but why did you refuse?"

Then Chairman Chung replied, beaming, "Dr Lee, do you think I'm a fool? Would Chairman Kubo propose something that wasn't beneficial to himself? When I heard what Chairman Kubo said, I was confident that the engine you've designed will succeed. So, work hard and make sure it succeeds."

---

4 Translator's note – In the 1980s, South Korea experienced a period of mass consumption, due to rapid economic growth, significant progress in industrial technology, and an increase in personal income. This led to the popularisation of 'my car', with car ownership becoming a popular consumption pattern and lifestyle among South Koreans.

Chairman Chung guffawed as he spurred me on. From then on, he fully supported the equipment expenses and research funding that the Mabuk Research Institute needed. He made clear his resolve to develop our own engine, even to the point of rejecting Mitsubishi's sweet offer.

The weight on my shoulders grew even heavier. I devoted myself fully to engine development while being subjected to the company's expectations and constraints. I couldn't allow the development of our own engine – a matter of life or death for Hyundai Motors – to fail.

19

I Shall Learn Despite Every Form of Humiliation

The process of engine development was easier said than done. As we had to begin everything new from the outset, there wasn't a single matter that we could glide over easily.

First we had to design an engine if we wanted to build one, but there was no one who could design an engine. Someone had to go abroad to study advanced technology. We signed a technical cooperation agreement with a British company called Ricardo. Ricardo, the founder of the eponymous company, had been the engine specialist who developed the most outstanding tank engine during the First World War. We decided to send a team to Ricardo to master the techniques of engine design.

The team left for the United Kingdom with the ambition to design engines properly. Ricardo gave the team a separate office. Two local employees were also with us, and they decided to teach us concept design. Ricardo was responsible for the initial concept design and computational analysis, and our team shared the work of producing a mass production design by developing detailed designs and prototypes. But Ricardo's employees weren't particularly friendly towards our team from a small country in Asia.

It happened when we were assigned an office after meeting with Ricardo's representatives on the first day. At one glance it was clear that the office was a shabby two-storey shed. A lunch prepared by Ricardo was ready on the shed's second floor, but there were only plastic-wrapped sandwiches and biscuits on an enormous tray. I figured that our employees shouldn't continue to be treated that way. I protested strongly to Ricardo's representatives.

"We came to the UK to work with you. But are you going to serve our employees, who have just arrived, with such cold food?"

Then their representatives brought us to the staff cafeteria. Only then could we have a proper meal. But they didn't change their attitude even after that. They tightly restricted our access so that we could enter only certain places, and they provided us with only shabby old tools for drawing our designs. We had to master the basics of design using tools that didn't fit our hands, and on old drawing boards. Ricardo and we had signed an agreement to jointly design an engine, but Ricardo employees were parsimonious about transferring their skills. With absolutely no prior experience in engine design, we were full of questions about everything related to design. When we asked questions, they kept their core technology secret and invariably answered evasively that they had simply learned from experience.

Amid such restrictions, we had to apply the techniques we learned each day by drawing the designs personally, all night long, mastering the techniques on our own. As we were inexperienced designers, our pace of learning the techniques was exceptionally slow. Over fifteen months, we gradually mastered the basics of designing while facing restrictions regarding accommodation, food and the copying of documents.

We completed a design after all this trouble, but the design we produced with Ricardo couldn't be commercialised right away. This was because the design hadn't taken into consideration the standards of South Korea's manufacturing technology or materials. Eventually, we could transform the design into specifications that could be manufactured in factories only after our design team had drastically revised the design three times to take account of our ability to produce and assemble it, and its cost competitiveness. Consequently, it became a wholly different engine from our initial design. In those days Ricardo was jointly developing engines with other companies too, but the only commercialised engine was the Alpha engine it had developed with us. If we hadn't possessed the will to succeed at all costs, it would have been impossible to develop an engine.

20

We Do Not Work with a Third-Rate Company

After designing an engine, you go through a phase of testing and production to make it commercially viable. This is called the trial production phase. We experienced considerable difficulties in the trial production phase too. At that time there were few South Korean companies that could produce the auto parts the Alpha engine needed. Though we intended to outsource the production of the auto parts, most companies couldn't even understand the specifications of the Alpha engine. The head of trial production had to visit each of the hundred and thirty or so component makers scattered across the entire country and persuade them.

"This time around Hyundai is developing the newest engine. We'd like to manufacture the engine's auto parts here. Can you manufacture them for us?"

The component makers then asked, "Why on earth do you want to develop an engine?"

Perhaps it was a predictable response, given that up to then no engine had been made in South Korea. The head of trial production then had to reiterate what he had already said multiple times to other companies: "Up till now, the engines that Hyundai has been using have been bought from Mitsubishi, but they aren't new products, so it'll be difficult for us to survive international competition in the future. We too must build the newest engine so we can compete on the global market, mustn't we?"

Then the component makers asked again, "If that's the case, what exactly is the engine that Hyundai has built?"

When the head of trial production explained the engine in detail, the component makers shook their heads.

"We would also have to invest a great deal to manufacture such an advanced engine. But if it's a prototype, won't you be ordering a variety of auto parts in small quantities? In that case, it won't be profitable for us. And if Hyundai gives up developing the engine midway, what do we do? This is a well-meaning idea, but it'll be difficult."

Our head of trial production had to take that all the time, in every company he visited. Though he visited component makers scattered across the country till blisters formed on his feet, there wasn't a company that was willing to produce the auto parts. He later earned the nickname 'record player', because he had called on countless companies and reiterated the same thing.

The prejudices of foreign companies were as difficult to deal with as those of South Korean companies. In particular, Mitsubishi harboured the belief, which bordered on confidence, that the Alpha engine would fail.

I once visited Japan on a business trip because there was an engine problem to discuss with Mitsubishi. Back then, Hyundai Motors was using Mitsubishi's Sirius engine, but it was hard for the engine to gain approval under the US anti-pollution law, so I convened a meeting with Mitsubishi's representatives. But as soon as I entered the meeting room, the director of research promptly said, "Creating an engine isn't that easy. I already knew that you'd come."

He spoke haughtily, and without even hearing me out, he continued: "However, if you want advice, you should have brought the Alpha engine. Why did you come empty-handed?"

He presumed that I had come to request help from Mitsubishi because of the Alpha engine. I told him confidently, "You don't have to worry about the Alpha engine. The reason I came is because of the Sirius engine, which Mitsubishi designed. You should know that the anti-pollution legislation has recently been strengthened in the United States. We're very worried, because it's difficult for the Sirius engine to meet US anti-pollution standards. I've come because I wanted to know how Mitsubishi plans to solve this problem."

The face of the director of research instantly contorted. He had intended to offer unwelcome advice about the Alpha engine, but his pride was hurt when I pinpointed the Sirius engine's problem. He stormed out of the room and didn't return, even after some time had passed. In the end, I discussed the problem with Mitsubishi's deputy director of research before returning to South Korea.

It was the same with overseas component makers. I thought we would unavoidably have to procure cutting-edge auto parts from overseas companies, even if we produced some of the engine parts in local companies. In the early stage of development, we planned to use the products of the German company Bosch. As the world's largest auto parts company back then, Bosch possessed exceptional technical skills. I had personally flown to Germany to buy Bosch's auto parts. But Bosch didn't believe me when I told them that we were building an engine independently.

"Are you saying that a small company like Hyundai is building an engine – something that even large companies have difficulty building?" the Bosch representative asked.

"That's right. We're now doing our best to build an engine with the newest specifications. We'll pay you any amount, so please send us the auto parts."

But the Bosch representative simply shook his head.

"We can barely produce the quantity for the large companies we're working with now. It'll be difficult for us to meet your orders, however much money you give us. How about working with companies like Lucas or Bendix?"

"What?" I asked, thinking I had heard him wrong. But the Bosch representative calmly replied, "We do not wish to work with a third-rate company like Hyundai."

What he said left me speechless. They might be a global company, but it made me boil with rage to suffer this humiliation. I firmly suppressed my anger and rose from my seat.

"If that's the case, it can't be helped. Please just know that you guys have missed out on a terrific opportunity."

Then, without changing his expression, he said, "I don't think we'll have any regrets."

We left Bosch without a fruitful outcome. No matter how much we talked about developing our own engine, no one listened. That was how low Hyundai Motors's popularity was. But we couldn't go back to South Korea just like that. It was only the beginning.

I pulled myself together and left to visit Lucas in the United Kingdom. Lucas was a much smaller company than Bosch. Back then, it was developing the system of the Japanese company Honda, but when I visited Lucas I found that its technical skills weren't especially superior. Therefore, I flew again to the United States, where Bendix was. Bendix was developing the auto parts for Chrysler's jeep cars, and I assessed that they had a certain level of technical skill. Only then did we sign an auto parts contract with Bendix and return to South Korea.

21

Building a Gearbox Independently Too

The gearbox is a core automobile technology that is as important as the engine. The gearbox is a device that transforms the power generated in an engine into the needed rotary power, which varies with speed. As with engines, Hyundai Motors was using gearbox technology from Mitsubishi too.

In those days, most automobile companies used twin-shaft gearboxes. A twin-shaft gearbox consists of two shafts: a drive shaft connected to the engine, and a relay shaft connected to the wheels. But interestingly, Mitsubishi used a three-shaft gearbox. Mitsubishi had developed the three-shaft gearbox on its own. Hyundai Motors was also using a three-shaft gearbox, because it was relying on Mitsubishi's technology. While we were developing our own engine, we had to decide on the gearbox too.

"Will we follow the global market trend and use a twin-shaft gearbox? Or will we go along with Mitsubishi's three-shaft gearbox?"

It would have been more convenient for us right then to go along with Mitsubishi's method of gearbox production. But it would be a different story if our production output were to increase subsequently. If things went wrong because we had adopted a production method different from global automobile market trends, we might become technologically subordinated to Mitsubishi. Taking the long view, it was a very risky decision.

After much consideration, we decided to also develop a gearbox suitable for the Alpha engine. In November 1984, several months after starting on the Alpha engine, we embarked on developing a manual gearbox for installation on the Alpha engine.

We were adamant about developing a gearbox on our own, but in reality there were a good many obstacles when we started. As with the development of the Alpha engine, there was no engineer in South Korea who had experience of developing a gearbox. Therefore, in the beginning we had to buy time because we couldn't recruit gearbox developers. Moreover, unlike engine design, there was nowhere we could learn the techniques for designing gearboxes. Our engineers had no choice but to face it directly and teach themselves to design gearboxes. We had to directly disassemble the Hyundai Pony's and Toyota's manual gearboxes, analyse them, and start to design gearboxes. All we had for reference were a few sample gearboxes and a gearbox drawing from Mitsubishi.

However, even if we could somehow develop the Alpha engine's manual gearbox by ourselves, it was impossible to design an automatic gearbox on our own. The difficulty of designing an automatic gearbox was greater than designing a manual one, and when we took into account the investment costs and timeline for engine development, it seemed better to buy the technology from other companies. However, eventually we reached a decision to design an automatic gearbox on our own and for technological independence. We settled on remodelling Mitsubishi's automatic gearbox into a two-shaft one. We decided to get Mitsubishi's help whenever we needed it while we drew the designs, but we had a difficult time because Mitsubishi guarded its designs closely – to the point of not accepting any questions on matters that were outside our contract.

As we hadn't yet established a systematic process for developing gearboxes, we had to enter a process where we first gave everything a shot and then corrected our mistakes. We repeated the process of generating numerous designs, creating a prototype, testing the prototype, analysing the test results, and then redesigning it. The number of gearboxes that we used for testing came to two hundred.

Our engineers handled this entire process mostly on their own, without external help. We went through this process and carried out the development of the Alpha engine and the gearbox step by step. Fortunately, the time it took to design the gearbox was shorter than for the engine, so it didn't cause a setback for the Alpha engine project.

Part 4

Inventing South Korea's First Automobile Engine

When someone devotes themselves fully to focusing on one thing, they can get brilliant ideas and make unthinkable discoveries. If you simply work hard like you usually do, there's nothing much you can achieve.

22

Why Does the Engine Keep Falling Apart?

The first engine prototype materialised on 26 October 1985. Seven months after we had started producing the prototype.

On the day we completed the first prototype, dozens of engineers who had participated in its production assembled in the research lab. We nervously placed a pig's head on the table and held a *gosa* ceremony.[5] Finally, the time came to test the prototype engine.

Will the engine work properly?
Surely nothing will go wrong?

I could sense both apprehension and hopefulness in the eyes of the engineers. Cautiously, we fired up the first prototype. Contrary to our apprehensions, the engine slowly picked up speed and ran powerfully. The engineers who were watching this cheered thunderously in the research lab. There were still numerous features that needed to be improved if we planned to

---

5 Translator's note – The *gosa* ceremony is a Korean shamanistic ritual aimed at warding off misfortune and bringing good luck. In Korean culture, pigs represent good fortune, money and fertility. The ceremony is sometimes held when Koreans move into a new house, start a new business, or buy a new car.

attain the performance we wanted. However, in that instant, we were delighted and awed simply by the fact that the engine we had designed actually worked.

Then almost one year later, in August 1986, we started the Alpha engine's durability testing. This was almost one and a half years after we had started designing it.

A durability test assesses how long an engine can operate robustly. Diverse forms of durability test are absolutely required to produce engines with outstanding performance. Besides, the engine we wanted to develop was quite a technologically outstanding engine. We needed repeated tests that went beyond ordinary development processes.

However, at the peak of durability testing in October, the prototype engines suddenly began to fall apart, one by one every week. In the past, the engines had also often fallen apart during the testing process. But each time we had found out the causes, corrected the problems and enhanced the performance. However, this time around it was different. We couldn't determine the causes, and the engines continued to fall apart. The entire research institute was in a state of crisis.

It cost more than twenty million won (approximately US$20,000) to produce a prototype engine. Today, producing a prototype engine requires a development cost of around one hundred million won (approximately US$100,000). This is because prototype engines aren't mass-produced but produced painstakingly, one by one, as if refining a work of art. As more than twenty engines had broken into pieces consecutively, not just one or two, our engineers were distressed.

There were diverse reasons why engines had fallen apart during the development process. Engines can fall apart because their designs have been drawn incorrectly, and there are also instances when engines fall apart because there is a problem with the testing method. There had been occasions when the engines broke into pieces because the component makers' technical skills were poor and they couldn't produce the engines properly based on our design specifications. Ever since we had started making up for the technical skills of the component makers, the number of engines that fell apart during durability testing had gradually decreased.

Sometimes engines fall apart because of absurd blunders. Usually, when you enter the research lab, you must open the cooling water line before operating the engine, and turn on the exhaust emission blower. Only then can the engine avoid overheating and operate normally. However, on one occasion, a research lab engineer forgot and started the engine without going through this process. Of course, the engine overheated and fell apart.

The face of the engineer, who realised this belatedly, turned deathly pale. He was suddenly struck with fear, because he had ruined an engine worth tens of thousands of dollars as a result of his blunder. Seized with fear and frustration, he went up the mountain behind the research institute, cried his eyes out, then came back down. I have never berated engineers over such incidents, but it was a fact that the engineers in our research institute shouldered such psychological burdens when building engines.

As soon as the rumour circulated that the Alpha engine was constantly falling apart, the criticisms and rebukes from people who had objected to the engine development gradually worsened.

"Look at that. Wouldn't it fail eventually?"

"Who will bear the responsibility, now that we have poured millions of dollars into developing a ridiculous engine?"

Whenever we heard these criticisms, a suffocating silence filled the research institute. Even I, who was confident in the Alpha engine, couldn't help but tense up. Two months passed, but there was absolutely no sign of us resolving the problem of the engine falling apart. We were distressed because we didn't even know the cause. At last, President Se-Yung Chung called for me.

"Dr Lee, don't you very well know how much money we are pouring into developing this engine? But is the engine only going to fall apart again and again? What exactly is the cause?"

But I couldn't say a word. I was the one, more than anyone else, who wanted to know why the engine was falling apart.

President Chung asked again, "Can we really produce the engine on our own?"

"I'm looking into the cause now. Please wait a little longer."

There was nothing else I could say.

23

Oh, Eureka!

Coming back to the research lab after meeting President Se-Yung Chung, I didn't express it outwardly, but inwardly I was fretting. I was indescribably depressed, looking at an engine that showed no sign of success and only fell apart. I wanted to find out the cause, no matter what it took.

I pulled myself together, entered the research lab and tried to start the engine. But it failed this time too. The engine, which had been operating well, overheated at one point and fell apart again. I felt all the strength drain out of my body.

Why on earth does it fall apart?

The Alpha engine had a relatively high thermal load, because it was a high-powered engine. Therefore, the head of the internal combustion cylinder often broke into pieces. Whenever that happened, we corrected the problems, one by one, but this time around we had no idea at all where the problem lay.

I picked up the broken engine and returned to my office. I placed each component on my desk and became lost in thought. It seemed that the cooling water couldn't cool down the engine. But I couldn't figure out which part of the engine had gone wrong and was obstructing the cooling water from flowing properly. I drew the structure of the engine in my head and started looking for defects.

The head of the cylinder is clearly the problem, so could its material be defective? Or have we designed it incorrectly?

I tried postulating every problem I could possibly think of, but none of them seemed to be the direct cause. I felt exasperated, as if I were wandering in the dark, because the engine to whose development I had devoted my heart and soul was hopelessly falling apart and I had no idea why. When I suddenly came to my senses, it was dark outside. It was eleven o'clock at night. I had returned to my office around four in the afternoon, which meant that I had been sitting and thinking for six to seven hours. I hurriedly prepared to knock off. But thoughts about the engine didn't leave my mind, even when I got home. I thought intently about the engine until I washed and went to bed, and then fell asleep without realising. I didn't stop thinking about the engine even in my dreams, and when I woke up hazily at dawn, it seemed that I had all of a sudden found the clue to solving the problem.

Could it be the bubbles?

The image of bubbles boiling in the cooling water appeared vividly before my eyes. It struck me that the cooling water might not be flowing well because of the bubbles that formed at the head of the cylinder. I hurriedly put on my clothes and left for the research lab. No one was in the lab, because it was early in the morning.

I calmed myself and tried to start the engine again. This time around I carefully observed the bubbles that formed at the head of the cylinder. What a surprise. As it happened, the cooling water could no longer flow properly as soon as the engine's temperature rose and the bubbles formed. Soon the engine could not withstand the overheating and broke into pieces. The bubbles were indeed the problem!

At long last, the cause of the engine failure, which had driven the entire Mabuk Research Institute into a crisis, was revealed as an 'abnormality with the cooling system', and we could look for clues to resolve it. It's said that scientists often find inspiration in their dreams when they are absorbed in a problem, and I happened to experience that too.

Most successful people know the power of immersion. They have delivered excellent results from the process of immersion. When someone devotes themselves fully to focusing on one thing, they can get brilliant ideas and make unthinkable discoveries. If you simply work hard like you usually do, there's nothing much you can achieve.

24

Failure Is Simply the Road to Success

The Alpha engine's trial production phase was never-ending. If we had been in a developed country that already had a technological foundation, we could have concluded the testing process with just a few dozen prototype engines. But we needed twenty to thirty prototype engines for the testing process alone. Of course, that wasn't all. We had to build around five hundred more prototype engines until we attained the specifications we desired.

Finally, the engine that had attained the desired specifications through trial and error was installed in a car and put through a testing process. As many as one hundred and fifty cars were used to test the Alpha engine. As the overall person in charge of the new engine development office, I personally drove the cars that were fitted with the Alpha engine, and I personally inspected specific problems like the noise and speed of the engine.

In order to develop an engine that can withstand extreme conditions, it's imperative to conduct not just local but overseas tests too. Tests that directly assess if an engine can withstand unimaginable heat or cold.

In July 1987, we tested the Alpha engine at a high temperature of forty-five degrees Celsius in Phoenix, Arizona, USA, together with engineers from the German company Bosch. When we conducted this high-temperature test in Phoenix, we had a close call, because the refrigerator truck had broken down and we had no idea at what point the fuel barrel might explode. In January 1988, we carried out a low-temperature test at minus thirty to forty degrees Celsius in Opasatika in the Canadian province of Ontario. In July 1989, we also carried out a high-altitude test in Denver, Colorado, at a height of one thousand six hundred metres and an atmospheric pressure of eight hundred and thirty millibars. All in all, I spent more than twenty-one thousand hours driving trial vehicles fitted with the engine. It was enough to have circled the earth a hundred and five times.

Finally, in 1991, Hyundai Motors succeeded in developing the 1.5-litre Alpha engine and a gearbox. It was six and a half years after we had started developing the engine.

People tell me that I'm a successful engineer, but I've encountered countless failures. When we were developing the Alpha engine, we had to newly build more than five hundred engines until we achieved the specifications we desired, and a hundred of them fell apart during the testing process. But even when failures reoccurred, I never abandoned the ultimate goal of developing an engine. That was because I knew for a fact that I couldn't develop the engine I wanted without repeating trial and error.

Failure is inevitable, because engineers do what others don't and create new things that the world doesn't have. Thomas Edison is renowned for having personally experimented with as many as one thousand six hundred heat-resistant materials and more than six thousand plant fibres to search out a material suitable for making filament. He tasted failure time and again during the process, but he never saw it as failure. He said that he hadn't failed at finding a material for making filament; he had succeeded in discovering materials that couldn't be used for making filament.

If you wish to become an outstanding engineer, you need a mental attitude that makes light of many such failures. You don't have what it takes to be an engineer if you become depressed and give up after one or two failures, I can assure you. You can succeed as an engineer only if you don't get cold feet in the face of failure. For an engineer, failure is simply the road to success.

25

The Jang Yeong Shil Award and Hospitalisation

The night after I returned from the press conference that informed the world about the Alpha engine, for the first time in a long while I looked back light-heartedly on the time that had passed. A period of more than six years, during which I had worked hectically on the engine, had flashed past like a *jooma deung*.[6] Everything looked like a scene from a movie: rushing to and fro to prepare a plot of land to construct the research institute, after I had first joined the company; recruiting employees for the research institute, and training them night after night; personally giving the name 'Alpha' to the new engine we were going to develop, and being absorbed in its development; and finally, presenting the engine to the world after conducting seemingly never-ending tests.

Around two hundred and fifty researchers had been deployed on the Alpha engine project. For a single project, it had deployed a very large number of researchers. Hundreds of engineers practically lived in the research labs for three hundred and sixty-five days a

---

6 Translator's note – A *jooma deung* is a zoetrope that generates images of running horses.

year, with the sole intention of developing our own engine. In a context where no one believed in the Alpha engine project, the project had been accomplished purely by the unyielding spirit and will of our engineers.

The performance of the Alpha engine was as remarkable as its symbolism as South Korea's very first automobile engine developed using our own technology. The engine's power output and fuel efficiency were appraised as far exceeding those of existing engines. That year, the Alpha engine was recognised for its technological superiority, and presented with the first Jang Yeong Shil Award. The Jang Yeong Shil Award is given to the development representative of a company or research institute that invents new technology, transforms that technology into products, and plays a leading role in South Korea's industrial technology innovation. For an engineer, nothing could be more rewarding than inventing South Korea's very first original engine and contributing to the advancement of the automobile industry. The Alpha engine's performance is so excellent that even today, more than twenty-three years after it was invented, it's still consistently used in places like China, Russia and South America. It has been discontinued in South Korea, but its total global production output has exceeded ten million.

However, what we gained from developing the Alpha engine wasn't simply the tangible outcome of having developed South Korea's very first engine. We learned a lesson more valuable than that. The lesson that technology can't be learnt from what people say or from books. Technology is something that can be acquired only from experience, through the process of constant trial and error.

In the process of developing the Alpha engine, little by little we could amass engine development know-how that was exclusive to us. This know-how wasn't something that we could have acquired by visiting a developed country, or by studying a great deal. It was something that we could obtain only through the process of personally experimenting with each idea and experiencing it ourselves. We could speed up subsequent engine development because we had this accumulated experience and technology. From then on, the Mabuk Research Institute could be reborn as the research institute that had spearheaded Hyundai Motors's technological development.

I tried to recall the faces of each engineer I had imperceptibly come to trust and depend on as if they were family. Mechanical engineering and heavy industry aren't sectors where a single genius can accomplish everything on their own. It would have been impossible to develop the Alpha engine if all the engineers at the research institute hadn't combined their efforts and given their all to develop it.

That night, I could sleep soundly – for the first time in a long while. But when I woke up the next morning, I couldn't move my body. My facial muscles were paralysed so I couldn't close my mouth or shut my eyelids. I was sent to the hospital right away.

"Looks like you've overworked your body all this while. Your immunity has weakened because of overwork, and an influenza virus has permeated your brain. For the time being, you should rest from work and take good care of your health."

That was the doctor's advice. Thanks to him, I was hospitalised for more than a month. Sprinting without resting for more than six years had taken a toll on my body.

All invention processes are the same, but inventing the Alpha engine in particular had created massive psychological pressure. It had been a project that drew severe objections from inside and outside the company, and the probability of succeeding had been exceedingly low. If the project had failed, it would certainly have devastated the company's future and sent hundreds of engineers, who had believed in and followed my lead, into the streets. As the head of the project, I hadn't wanted to give young and promising engineers the experience of failure. Therefore, I hadn't shown it, but I had felt immense pressure to succeed. As soon as I had completed the engine, I was relieved of tension all at once, and I fell sick. Thankfully, when I was hospitalised, I somewhat recovered from the paralysis. However, even now, the after-effects of that paralysis remain on my face.

26

Even Chairman Kubo Gave Us Recognition

It happened around the time when we had succeeded with the Alpha engine and were focusing on constructing factories that could mass-produce it. One day, Chairman Kubo from Mitsubishi visited South Korea. This time he came to meet me, not Chairman Chung. As soon as he stepped into the Mabuk Research Institute, Chairman Kubo looked for me.

"Who is Dr Hyun-Soon Lee? I'd like to meet Dr Lee."

When I appeared before him, he greeted me warmly.

"I hear that you led the invention of the Alpha engine. If it's all right, may I look at the engine?"

I gladly ushered him to the research lab. On our way to the lab, he asked: "I've been inventing engines all my life too. Therefore, when you said you were going to create an engine, that hit close to home. So, what was the most difficult thing you faced when you were building the engine?"

I replied frankly, "The most difficult thing when building a high-performance engine was to minimise heat deflection."

Then Chairman Kubo nodded his head as if he understood.

"I also had a hard time when I was building the Zero fighter aircraft during the Second World War because of the engine's severe heat deflection."

We soon felt that we could connect. He was asking me questions as an engineer, not as the head of a rival company.

"It can't have been easy adjusting the heat deflection temperature. How much of the engine's temperature difference did you control?"

"At first, we aimed to reduce the temperature to no more than eighty degrees Celsius. We couldn't reduce it that much, but we could reduce it to ninety-two degrees Celsius."

When I said that, he looked surprised. That was understandable, because the temperature difference that caused heat deflection in most engines at that time was typically a hundred degrees Celsius. It was remarkable that the Alpha engine could reduce the heat deflection temperature to ninety-two degrees Celsius. But I was disappointed that we hadn't met our original goal.

"How did you measure the temperature difference?"

"Well, we measured it with a thermometer."

Then Chairman Kubo said that he wanted to see the engine quickly. I showed him the engine that was kept in the research lab. The engine, which had been fully developed, had around two hundred and forty thermometers densely stuck all over it. Chairman Kubo was awestruck after studying the engine carefully, and he said, "This is really incredible. If you want to build a good engine, you must devote this amount of effort. I'm truly delighted to meet a brilliant engineer like you."

I was doubtful of Chairman Kubo's excessive praise.

"Don't you do the same at Mitsubishi?"

"Mitsubishi doesn't do this. In order to minimise heat deflection, we build thick engines from the start."

"In that case, doesn't their performance decline? Can you compete on the global market with such engines?"

Chairman Kubo smiled bitterly at what I had said.

"That's the problem."

It had been Chairman Kubo who had tried hard to dismiss me in order to stop Hyundai Motors developing its own engines, but he was a born engineer too. Having devoted his entire life to building good engines, he gave his recognition as an engineer to our technical skill in producing the Alpha engine.

I heard this later, but Chairman Kubo rushed straight to Mitsubishi's research institute in Okazaki as soon as he returned to Japan. He convened more than a thousand Mitsubishi engineers in an auditorium.

"I just came back from South Korea. I visited Hyundai Motors, and they have a very tenacious engineer. If all of us don't get our act together, we might have to go to Hyundai Motors to master their technical skills in ten years' time. Therefore, please develop new technology diligently."

Mitsubishi's researchers couldn't leave work that day, and they had to listen to Chairman Kubo lecturing for hours. But no one believed all that Chairman Kubo said. That was because even as he was delivering his warning to them, the engine production team at Hyundai Motors's Ulsan factory was still acquiring technology from Mitsubishi. However, astonishingly, a few years later, Chairman Kubo's warning became a reality.

27

We Want to Partner with Hyundai

Even after inventing the Alpha engine, we didn't rest on our laurels, and we sped up our subsequent engine development work. Hyundai Motors's technical skills were improving by the day. Our status on the global automobile market was rising too. The Hyundai Excel, which succeeded the Hyundai Pony, was well received in the United States. The fact that Hyundai Motors was investing heavily in engine development became known, and the perspectives of overseas companies began to change noticeably. The change in Bosch's attitude, in particular, was memorable.

The attitude of Bosch, which had slammed the door in our face when we were inventing the Alpha engine, had transformed entirely in a few years. Bosch conveyed its intention to jointly develop engine components with us.

"Until now, Bosch hasn't partnered with any other company. But we'd like to form a partnership with Hyundai."

But I didn't forget the humiliation we had suffered a few years before. I had absolutely no intention to work with Bosch, which had called us a third-rate company. Therefore, I replied, "Thank you for the offer, but we've already contracted with other companies for the components we need. I'm sorry, but please look for another company."

But they didn't give up easily. This time around they informed President Se-Yung Chung of their intention to work with us. President Chung convened Bosch's executives and representatives from our research institute in one place, and said, "I don't know anything about engine development. I simply do it if Dr Lee says do it, and don't do it if Dr Lee says not to. Therefore, it's better to first persuade Dr Lee."

Only then did Bosch's chairman take a step back.

"All right. In that case, let's take the time to discuss this partnership slowly, and please visit our company as soon as you can. I'd like to show you all the products and technology that we are developing."

Bosch was the company that had supplied auto parts to Benz when the latter invented the first automobile in Germany in 1886. That meant that Bosch was proud of its technology. I didn't have a fond impression of Bosch personally, but I was secretly curious about its technology. Therefore, I made time to visit Bosch's research institute in Germany. As expected, Bosch was an outstanding company. It wasn't an overstatement to say that in terms of both technical skills and scale, Bosch and Benz were prominent players in the industry and global pioneers of automobile technology. Perhaps Bosch had expected me to change my mind after seeing its outstanding technical skills for myself. However, after the visit, I said, "I know that your company is great. But I still can't decide whether we should collaborate or not. Let's talk about this again next time."

Then I returned to South Korea without looking back.

However, not long after my visit to Bosch, we abruptly heard from Mitsubishi that it could no longer supply us with auto parts. Back then, Hyundai Motors was using a fueller for the Hyundai Excel that was supplied by Mitsubishi. Without the fueller, we couldn't export the Hyundai Excel to the United States. Taken aback by Mitsubishi's unexpected announcement, we looked into its reason for doing so and realised that Bosch had meddled in the matter.

Mitsubishi was producing the fueller for the Hyundai Excel using patented technology originally developed by Bosch. But Bosch had pressured Mitsubishi into not supplying the fueller to Hyundai Motors. Bosch owned the original technology, so Mitsubishi couldn't supply us with the device even if it wanted to.

In the automobile business, it is of paramount importance to possess original technology. If you don't possess original technology, you must pay royalties to companies that do possess it whenever you manufacture automobiles. Hyundai Motors had also invested astronomical amounts and developed our own engine in order to possess original technology. That was because if we didn't possess original technology, we would have no choice but to eventually become subordinated to a company that did possess it – and this was how we could be spun around by Mitsubishi.

After pressuring Mitsubishi, Bosch notified us: "In future, we shall directly supply the auto parts for the Hyundai Excel. But we have one condition: you must partner with us if you want to receive the auto parts."

We were caught in a dilemma. If we didn't collaborate with Bosch, we couldn't receive the relevant auto parts, and so we couldn't export the Hyundai Excel to the United States. We had to export the cars. But unhappy about working with Bosch, I continued to stall for time, even though I had decided to work with them. We had nothing to lose this time around, so we were fastidious about the conditions for the partnership. Nevertheless, Bosch accepted all our conditions. Finally, after one and a half years, we formed a joint venture. Unlike our treatment when we first visited Bosch, we could now negotiate conditions that we were satisfied with, because Hyundai Motors had gained in stature.

28

The Misfortunate Gamma Engine

Hyundai Motors's engine development, which had started with the Alpha engine, continued smoothly with the Theta engine, Lambda engine and Tau engine. Every engine is dear to us, because we developed all of them painstakingly. It sufficed to feel a sense of pride in the fact that the Alpha engine had been the very first engine developed domestically, though no one had believed that we would succeed. It was especially meaningful that Hyundai's technical skills became globally recognised because of the Theta engine and the Tau engine. However, among all these, there is an engine that holds special meaning for me, and that is the Gamma engine. As soon as we succeeded in inventing the Alpha engine and the Beta engine, our team started designing the Gamma engine as an engine for mid-sized passenger cars.

Mitsubishi was constantly looking out for opportunities to stop us developing our own engines. When I had been dismissed from my post, Mitsubishi had deployed our competent engineers to remodel its Orion engine. Mitsubishi had wanted to jointly develop engines with Hyundai in that way. The reason was that it was entirely favourable to Mitsubishi to do so. From Mitsubishi's standpoint, it was killing two birds with one stone, because

Mitsubishi could deploy our engineers to remodel its engines, and it could register the patents under the pretext of providing technical guidance. While our engineers were developing Mitsubishi's engines, Hyundai Motors's development of our own engines was inevitably delayed. The remodelling of the Orion engine fortunately fell through when I was reinstated as the director of the new engine development office, but even after that, Mitsubishi constantly strove to stop us developing our own engines.

It all happened while Hyundai Motors was designing the 2,000 cc and 2,400 cc models of the Gamma engine. In those days, we had secured the technology for developing our own engines, but we couldn't yet become fully independent in gearbox technology. For that reason, we had to acquire Mitsubishi's newest gearbox technology and modify it before using it. Mitsubishi had developed a new gearbox for mid-sized passenger cars around that time, so we considered acquiring and using that technology. But Mitsubishi didn't plan to give us the technology easily.

"We've a condition for you if you want to use our newest gearbox technology. We've just remodelled the Sirius engine and developed the Sirius II engine, and we want to offer technical support by bundling our newest gearbox technology with the Sirius II engine. How's that?"

If we were to use Mitsubishi's Sirius II engine, the Gamma engine, whose designs we had so painstakingly completed, would become useless.

"The performance of the Gamma engine is better than the Sirius II engine's. We can't give up on the Gamma engine because of the gearbox."

I firmly opposed Mitsubishi's proposal, but they had persuaded our board of directors on various points.

"Hyundai is already using the Sirius engine, so surely there's no need to build new factories if you use the Sirius II engine? It's a favourable decision for Hyundai Motors too, because you can save on factory investments as well."

Mitsubishi had a point. Performance was important when developing engines, but we also had to consider cutting production costs. Moreover, if we wanted to use Mitsubishi's gearbox technology, we needed to accept something of their proposal.

In those days, Hyundai Motors's engine technology had risen to a significant level, but our gearbox technology was still poor. Of course we could design a manual gearbox for the Alpha engine, but designing an automatic gearbox was different. As we didn't fully possess the technology to design an automatic gearbox, realistically it was difficult to turn down Mitsubishi's proposal. I objected to the end, but our board of directors eventually took Mitsubishi's side.

The Gamma engine, which our engineers had painstakingly designed, was buried without seeing the light of day. It makes an engineer very frustrated to have to abandon an engine that they have poured their heart and soul into designing. Whenever I saw the Gamma engine, which we had ceased developing and which slept peacefully in one corner of the research lab, my heart ached. As an engineer I was even more upset, because nothing about the Sirius II engine was better than the Gamma engine.

From then on, I was even more determined to raise our standards to world-class level, whether in engine technology or gearbox technology. If we couldn't prevail over rival companies technologically, there was no guarantee that the same thing wouldn't repeat itself in future. I soon began to conceptualise the newest engine that would surpass Mitsubishi's in every way. I also substantially strengthened our gearbox technology. I didn't want to create another case of misfortune like the Gamma engine.

29

Finally, Royalties!

Regrettably, the Gamma engine didn't see the light of day, but Mitsubishi's obstructions couldn't stop our passion for developing engines. We improved the performance of the Gamma engine substantially, and carried out an ambitious plan to build an engine that surpassed the Sirius engine.

Hyundai Motors had established the Mabuk Research Institute in 1984, and developed the Alpha engine – our first original engine – after about seven years. It took four years to develop our second engine, called the Beta engine. After the Beta engine, we practically released one new engine every year, but there was a slight time gap in developing the Theta engine. We devoted our heart and soul to boosting the performance of the Theta engine. The sixth gasoline engine developed by Hyundai Motors, the Theta engine was an ambitious piece of work that was presented thirteen years after we had succeeded in inventing the Alpha engine.

The Alpha engine had been the very first automobile engine we had developed on our own, but the Theta engine was significant to us – who were always tirelessly catching up with advanced technology – because we became recognised on the global market for our technical skills thanks to it. It was significant because

Hyundai Motors, which had used engine technology bought from other companies, was now transferring its own design technology to other companies for the first time.

We could transfer the Theta engine's technology to global automobile companies because, for the most part, the engine's design was exceptionally outstanding. But there was a backstory about the engine that wasn't widely known, even within Hyundai Motors.

When the 1997 Asian financial crisis broke out and the South Korean government was actively seeking foreign capital, Benz acquired ten percent of Hyundai Motors's shares. In those days, Benz was operating its business aggressively, and it had already taken over Chrysler and Mitsubishi. It was waiting eagerly for an opportunity to do the same to Hyundai Motors. As a form of collaboration, Benz suggested that Hyundai and Benz should exchange top executives. I happened to be chosen, and I maintained an amicable relationship with Benz's employees. Benz then presented me with a proposal.

"Benz is developing a small four-seater car called the Smart car this time around, and as you know, Benz has almost never built a small engine. We'd like Hyundai to design a small engine for the Smart car. How's that?"

It was a fine proposal.

"Designing a small engine won't be difficult, because we've designed countless small engines since the Alpha engine. I'll make time to look at it."

I replied positively that I'd review their proposal, but I couldn't design the Smart engine because I was swamped with other projects. This time Benz proposed: "Regarding the engine we spoke to you about last time. We'd like Hyundai to not just design but also supply the entire engine. How's that?"

This time I was enticed by their proposal. If we could produce and supply the engine directly, and not simply hand over the engine design, we could expect ample profits. I agreed readily and occupied myself with developing the Smart engine in earnest.

One day, the headquarters chief – who was my superior – came to me.

"Benz has requested a small engine, hasn't it? Can I look at the material costs?"

I couldn't trust this headquarters chief, who had suddenly said that he wanted to look at the engine's material costs, but it was hard to refuse a superior's order. But the fact that the headquarters chief was close to Mitsubishi weighed on my mind. I received a firm assurance from him.

"I'll show it to you because you want to look at it. But keep this an absolute secret from Mitsubishi and Benz. Please keep it to yourself."

"All right," said the headquarters chief, who then took with him the quotation sheet with the material costs.

Sometime later, I was waiting for Benz's reply after completing the Smart engine's design and sending them the quotation, when I heard an absurd rumour: Mitsubishi was developing Benz's small engine. I went to Benz's top executives.

"I heard that Mitsubishi is developing Benz's small engine. Is that true?"

Then they turned ghastly pale and looked evasive. Only then did I grasp the situation.

"How could you do this? To our face you called us a partner, and then behind our backs you're making Mitsubishi and us compete? Is this what a partner would do?"

Benz had asked not just Hyundai Motors but Mitsubishi too to design the engine for the Smart car. In other words, they intended to entrust the engine's production to whichever company – Hyundai Motors or Mitsubishi – presented the better terms. Instead of a partner, they had regarded us as no different from a supplier. I was livid.

"You've no right to be our partner. Please sell the shares you have right now and leave. We'll buy the shares back."

"We're very sorry. It wasn't our intention to…"

"Wasn't your intention to do what? I don't want to speak to any of you any more, so please don't visit us again in future," I said, then walked away without looking back.

Even after I returned to my office, my anger didn't go away easily. I was disgusted by how Benz had treated us as a supplier, but what made me angrier was the fact that my quotation sheet for the Smart engine had fallen into Mitsubishi's hands. I had obtained the headquarters chief's assurance, but he had handed our quotation sheet over to Mitsubishi. Mitsubishi had studied our quotation sheet thoroughly, and presented Benz with a quotation at a slightly lower price. Therefore, the development of the Smart engine had been bound to fall into Mitsubishi's hands. The more I thought about it, the angrier I got.

After all the commotion, I devoted myself to the next project right away. The Theta engine. The Theta engine was an ambitious piece of work that might become a new turning point for domestically produced engines. We had already succeeded in developing the Alpha and Beta engines, but I hadn't forgotten the sense of frustration I had experienced because of the Gamma engine. I didn't want to be pressured by Mitsubishi into burying our technology again. To ensure this, we had to create an engine that surpassed Mitsubishi's in every respect. If the new engine gave good performance but poor fuel efficiency, or if it gave good performance and fuel efficiency but demanded high investment costs, it could give Mitsubishi a reason to pressure us again. It was not enough for the Theta engine to stand out in one respect only. I wanted an engine that surpassed Mitsubishi's in every respect. Therefore, I made this request of my engineers:

"The Theta engine will be an engine that stands out in every respect. Please design it so that its performance is exceptional and its production costs are low. We must also reduce factory investment costs, so you must ensure that the engine can be produced using the processing machinery in the Ulsan engine factory."

In short, I aimed to produce the engine using the highest standard of technology but the lowest development costs. The engineers became tense at my request. It was a more difficult mission than ever. But they knew what I thought – that we would surpass Mitsubishi in every respect only if we could pull this off. We were like-minded on this desperate goal, and we occupied ourselves solely with developing the Theta engine.

When the Theta engine's design was almost completed, Benz's director of engine development visited me out of the blue. He was a friend I had known for a long time, since we had met by chance at an international conference while I was studying for my doctoral degree. Born engineers, we had a close relationship, as we would freely call one another and seek each other's opinion if we had any questions during the process of developing engines.

He asked: "I hear that Hyundai Motors has recently been developing a high-performance engine. Can I take a look at it?"

"Why do you want to look at it?"

"Actually, our company is looking for a way to work with Hyundai Motors, so I'd like to see if the engine you're developing now is fit for use. Looks like our board of directors has been quite troubled since they made things difficult for you the other time because of the Smart engine."

"Really? If that's the intention, there's nothing I can't show you. I'll trust you and show it to you because you're my friend."

I readily showed him the Theta engine's design. He was also an expert who would feel sad if he came second place in engine design. After he had closely studied the engine's design and specifications, he said with a look of satisfaction, "The engine has been very well designed. Even if Benz were to design it, we probably couldn't design better than this."

After he had returned to his company, he sent me a letter. He wrote that Benz needed a mid-sized engine and wanted to jointly use the Theta engine. Back then, both Chrysler and Mitsubishi were Benz subsidiaries. Therefore, we naturally entered an agreement to transfer the technology for installing the Theta engine into automobiles produced by Chrysler and Mitsubishi. It was a historic moment: exporting our technology – through the Theta engine – to the United States, the birthplace of the automobile, and Japan, which was leading the world's automobile industry. Having busied ourselves keeping up with advanced technology, we had finally arrived at a stage where we took the lead in technology. With this agreement, we received US$57 million in royalties.

But I wasn't satisfied. When we drafted the agreement, we laid down strict conditions. There was a condition stipulating that my approval had to be sought if the engine's design was modified. I had my reasons for including this condition. When three companies jointly produce an engine, it's possible to mass-produce the relevant auto parts. If Hyundai produced six hundred thousand engines, and if, as the result of a collaboration between three companies, 1.8 million engines were concurrently produced worldwide, we could reduce the cost price of the relevant auto parts by around ten percent. By stipulating in the agreement that no one could modify the Theta engine's design without permission, we could expect not only royalties, but also additional profits as a result of reducing the cost price of auto parts production.

No doubt it's a fact that the efforts of Benz, which had lost our trust in the process of designing the Smart engine, played a role in the Theta engine's global expansion. However, above all, the biggest reason for the Theta engine's global expansion was that its performance was so outstanding that it couldn't be beaten, no matter where it was used in the world. If the Theta engine's design hadn't been outstanding, the technology transfer agreement wouldn't have materialised, even if Benz had wanted it to.

30

Welcome, Dr Lee – Father of the World Engine!

We had started developing the Theta engine with the aim to substantially improve the specifications of the Gamma engine and produce a small, light engine. For that reason, we made countless new attempts: first we significantly reduced the engine's weight by creating its body, previously made of cast iron, out of aluminium. Then we implemented an electronically controlled state-of-the-art system that groundbreakingly reduced fuel and power usage. Dissatisfied, we strove to reduce the engine's noise, even as we worked on boosting its performance. In short, the Theta engine was an engine that had high levels of fuel efficiency and noise reduction, as well as exceptional durability.

Around a hundred and forty researchers spent a total of almost four years devoting themselves fully to developing the Theta engine. We used around four hundred prototype engines, and experienced two fires that set our research labs aflame due to engine overheating. As with the development of the Alpha engine, our engineers resided in the labs and poured in all their passion while we were developing the Theta engine.

Chairman Mong-Gu Chung, who was head of Hyundai Motors at the time, had enormous interest in the Theta engine too. That was because the Theta engine was going to be fitted on the Hyundai Sonata. It is no overstatement to say that in those days the Sonata was the pride of Hyundai. It was the car model that we concentrated the most on selling in the United States. It went without saying that we had little choice but to pay far more attention to its quality assurance than to that of any other car.

Despite his hectic schedule, Chairman Mong-Gu Chung stopped by the research institute once a month to raise the morale of the engineers in the research labs. He liked to say this to the engineers: "We must secure the quality of an automobile in its development phase. It costs us one dollar to secure its quality at an early stage, but this cost rises to ten dollars if we try to fix its problems in the process of mass-producing it. This cost increases to a hundred dollars if we have to recall automobiles that are already being sold on the market, or if we have to provide after-sales servicing. Therefore, no matter what, please sift out all the problems right from the development phase."

The Theta engine's development team had to suffer several times more than other teams, because the company strove for perfection right from the development phase. Even so, the management team didn't gloss over anything. Whenever the development team released a finished product, thinking that we were somewhat done, the finished product was always returned by the quality assurance department. Even when the new Hyundai Sonata's launch date was approaching, the management team didn't release its final appraisal of the engine. We were in a situation where if things went wrong, we would have to postpone the launch date we had promised the media.

In order to meet the launch date, the development team gave up their rest days and worked to correct the engine's defects. The quality assurance department had pointed out that the engine produced a very slight noise for around five seconds when the engine was started in temperatures below minus ten degrees Celsius. We corrected this with piston configuration, then sent the Theta engine back to the quality control department again, and waited for the results. All our engineers were utterly exhausted. We were waiting anxiously for the results, but the quality assurance department's notification came later than expected. We had mixed emotions: anticipation that the engine would be approved this time, and anxiety that perhaps the engine might be returned to us yet again. If the engine was disqualified again this time around, we would have no choice but to postpone the Hyundai Sonata's launch date.

As tension lingered in the research institute, the quality assurance department finally relayed their response. It was approved! The final appraisal stated that the Theta engine's performance and quality would receive positive reviews on any market in the world. Only now could our engineers take a breather and fully rejoice.

The Theta engine, which we had devoted our heart and soul to developing, was fitted on the NF Sonata. And it received more positive reviews than expected. In the United States too, the Theta engine was reviewed as an engine that was technically highly developed.

In September 2005, Mitsubishi completed the construction of a factory at its Kyoto production plant that was built exclusively to produce four hundred thousand Theta engines. It then started producing the Theta engine in earnest. Mitsubishi planned to install the Theta engine on 1,800 cc to 2,400 cc automobiles.

In October the same year, Chrysler completed the construction of an engine factory in Dundee, Michigan, United States, that could produce four hundred and twenty thousand engines yearly. And in November the same year, they also planned to construct a second factory beside the first Dundee factory, to produce a total of eight hundred and forty thousand Theta engines.

When Chrysler invested one trillion won (US$1 billion) in constructing engine factories, I visited the United States at its invitation. As soon as I alighted from the car, all the factory workers came out to welcome me. On a placard that hung from the top of the factory was written: 'Welcome, Dr Lee – Father of the World Engine!'

The name of the Theta engine that Chrysler and Mitsubishi were using was none other than 'world engine'. As the name suggested, the Theta engine had become a universal engine. *Motor Trend*, a well-known automobile magazine in the United States, said this of the Theta engine:

> *Each year, Daimler-Chrysler, Mitsubishi and Hyundai Motors produce between 1.5 and 2 million 1,800 cc, 2,000 cc and 2,400 cc Theta engines. According to Automotive Intelligence News, this figure is the highest in the world for automobile engines.*

Hyundai, Chrysler and Mitsubishi jointly produced the Theta engine, and it became the most produced single engine in a year.

We produced 1.84 million engines in 1997 alone, and this record hasn't been broken.

Mitsubishi and Hyundai Motors had been partners who formed technical partnerships and worked together, depending on our respective needs. But it had primarily been a partnership where technology was transferred from Mitsubishi to Hyundai Motors. This was entirely reversed with the development of the Theta engine. Fully technologically independent, Hyundai Motors now transferred engine technology to Mitsubishi. After experiencing the frustration of the Gamma engine, we turned that experience into a force for growth. As we didn't cling to failures, and we constantly challenged ourselves, we finally leaped from being a second mover to a front runner who takes the lead in technology.

Chrysler's and Mitsubishi's engineers visited Hyundai Motors's engine research institute to receive technical training on the Theta engine for three months at a time. When they were constructing production factories for the Theta engine, we sent out three of our engineers at a time to supervise the construction, and we provided technical guidance for four years. The warning that Chairman Kubo had issued to Mitsubishi's engineers after touring the Mabuk Research Institute ten years before had become a reality at last. And even now, more than ten years after the development of the Theta engine, Chrysler and Mitsubishi are still using it. Sixty percent of the automobiles that Chrysler produces, such as the Chrysler Jeep and the Chrysler PT Cruiser, and seventy percent of Mitsubishi's automobiles are still travelling the world installed with the Theta engine. The Theta engine was a splendid feat that showed how Hyundai had risen from a second mover to a front runner in the automobile industry, and how Hyundai's technical skills had reached world-class standards.

Hyundai Motors didn't rest on its laurels, and it further expedited its engine development work. In 2008, after the development of the Alpha engine, Beta engine and Theta engine, a full line-up of engines was formed with the release of the Tau engine, seventeen years after the Alpha engine had been launched. Our engine development know-how had progressed beyond a certain level.

Hyundai Motors's standard of engine technology is now on par with any automobile company in the world. In particular, the Tau engine that was released in 2008 was awarded WardsAuto's Top Ten Best Engines – the Academy Award of the automobile engine sector – for three consecutive years, and recognised for its technical skill. WardsAuto, which started in 1994, is the most prestigious award in the engine sector. It assesses the bestselling engine models in North America every year and gives an award to the most outstanding engine. If we consider that Hyundai Motors had been a company that bought engine technology about twenty years before, becoming a recipient of this award showed that we had achieved extraordinary progress. Moreover, in 2009 the Hyundai Genesis, which was installed with the Tau engine, had the honour of being chosen as South Korea's very first 'North American Car of the Year'.

31

Why Can't You Make Electric Vehicles?

I'm a born engineer who likes smearing my hands with oil grease and living in the research lab with other engineers. But time passed and I slowly found myself in a position where I needed to make important decisions. Subsequently, I led the research and development department, which was responsible for developing new automobiles.

When I was overseeing research and development, I kept my eyes not just on engines, but on the market for next-generation automobiles as well, so that I could understand the market beforehand and develop automobiles that were slightly more competitive. In those days, the entire global automobile industry was interested in hybrid cars. Hybrid cars, in short, refer to environmentally friendly futuristic cars. They are cars that either use lesser petrol than existing cars or adopt new energy sources like electricity or hydrogen gas to innovatively reduce car exhaust fumes.

Even now, automobile companies around the world are competing fiercely to develop better-performing hybrid cars. I had also predicted that the future of the automobile industry lay in hybrid cars. I thought that perhaps hybrid cars would account for fifteen percent of the entire world's automobiles by around 2020.

But I figured that it was still difficult for electric vehicles to be commercialised in South Korea. There were several reasons, but first it was due to the high production cost of the batteries used for electric vehicles. Even if they were environmentally friendly cars, it would be difficult to commercialise them if they weren't priced competitively. In addition, the long charging time for the batteries of electric vehicles, and the need to set up charging stations across the country, were also issues. And eight more nuclear power stations would have to be built to supply the electricity that electric vehicles would need. In many respects, electric vehicles weren't yet realistic.

On the other hand, prospects for hydrogen-powered electric vehicles in South Korea were bright. In countries like South Korea, where steel mills and oil refineries are numerous, five million hydrogen-powered cars could roam around if they obtained only twenty percent of the hydrogen gas emitted by these facilities. Moreover, hydrogen was sufficiently economically viable, because it was far cheaper than petrol. But the media and television, which had an inadequate understanding of this technology, weren't interested in such alternatives. They simply asked why Hyundai Motors wasn't producing electric vehicles. Once, the director of the Blue House's future planning office called on me with his employees. He asked me why automobile companies in developed countries had foreseen the future and developed electric vehicles but Hyundai Motors had not.

I replied, "Building electric vehicles is technically not a very hard thing to do. In reality, electric vehicles were being built even in the 1890s. All we need are motors and batteries, so there's no reason why we can't make them. In fact, they are far easier to make than cars installed with engines. Hyundai isn't making electric vehicles because they are impractical, not because we lack the technology to make them."

But it seemed they couldn't understand me.

"Why are they impractical?"

"The production cost of electric vehicles is high. Though they are environmentally friendly cars, no one will buy them if they are costly. And charging stations would have to be built in every corner of the country for electric vehicles to move around, but does the government intend to build *that* many charging stations?" I retorted.

But they didn't take my word for it. They seemed to think that we were making up excuses because we couldn't make electric vehicles. Therefore, one year later, we developed an electric car and presented it at the Blue House. We directly showed them that it wasn't because we couldn't build electric vehicles. The president himself even did a test drive of the electric car we had made. Highly satisfied, the president asked, "How many more of this car can you make?"

"We can make as many as you like."

The government then ordered two hundred and thirty electric vehicles. Quietly, I asked, "We can make them, but where exactly do you plan to use them?"

The reason I asked was that no matter how many electric vehicles there were, they would be practically useless if there were no charging stations. They said that they would give the electric vehicles to government agencies and local governments for official use. The orders came, so we started making them right away. However, even after we had built all the cars they had ordered, the government delayed day after day, without collecting the cars.

"Why haven't you collected the cars you ordered?"

Then they replied, "Looks like it'll be difficult to use them right now, because charging stations haven't been constructed yet. Please wait a little longer."

Consequently, two hundred and thirty electric vehicles had to be left untouched, standing on the test site of our research lab, for more than a year. The government realised that electric vehicles weren't feasible only after ignoring the direct words of an engineer and directly producing the vehicles.

In a technology-based society, it's difficult to formulate the right policies without a correct understanding of technology. Therefore, leaders of a country ought to understand technology before they formulate policies.

32

Without Our Own Technology

In 1999, Hyundai Motors started developing hybrid cars. The Japanese company Toyota had started developing hybrid cars before we did. We had to hurry.

The interesting thing was that we faced similar objections to developing hybrid cars as we had encountered when we had started to develop the Alpha engine. When I said that we were going to develop hybrid cars using our own technology, my direct superior said: "Looks like it'll be difficult to develop hybrid cars using our own technology… How about forming a technical partnership with Toyota instead?"

I felt like I was hitting a brick wall once again. In a manufacturing business like the automobile business, it's of paramount importance to secure original technology in one's core field before the competitors do. This is why patent wars over core technology occur frequently. Toyota had a considerable number of company patents, having started developing hybrid cars first. It wasn't an easy task to avoid Toyota's patents, which were as densely intertwined as a cobweb, and develop hybrid cars using our own technology. For that reason, there were some people who thought it would be better to buy Toyota's technology than to laboriously develop our own technology. They didn't want to risk it. Not that I wasn't aware of that fact.

But I said firmly, "It's a fact that Toyota started developing hybrid cars before we did. But there's no reason why we shouldn't develop hybrid cars because of that. Why must we buy Toyota's technology?"

I was confident that we could develop hybrid cars on our own, and I went ahead with it. It was also a matter of my pride as an engineer.

However, we faced numerous difficulties as soon as we started developing them. There was no company in South Korea that could produce auto parts for hybrid cars. The companies lacked the technical skills, and none was keen to work with us because our scale of development was small. It was the same situation as had happened when we were developing the Alpha engine. We reluctantly looked for Japanese component makers. Fortunately, we could jointly develop the components with several companies that were working with Toyota. Now it was just a matter of fully mobilising the technology and speeding up the development process. Then it happened.

"We regret to inform you that we are unable to supply Hyundai with the components due to our company's situation."

Japan's component makers – such as Sanyo, which produced batteries, and Hitachi, which produced motors – notified us, one after the other, that they were terminating their contracts with us. If our contracts were terminated, all that we had developed over the past few years would go to waste.

Hurriedly, I contacted Japan's component makers. I had to avert the worst-case scenario. But there was nothing we could do. It was because of Toyota's obstruction.

In the automobile business, where companies must stay ahead in technology, keeping rival companies in check is a commonplace thing. When it came to developing hybrid cars, Toyota and we were competitors. It turned out that Toyota's chairman had convened all the leaders of the component-making companies and notified them that they couldn't work with Toyota if they continued to work with Hyundai. As Japanese component makers, it was difficult for them to disregard Toyota's notification. In the end, we had to comprehensively revise our development of hybrid cars, which we had carried out for four years, as a result of Toyota's plain obstruction. The source of our trouble was being overly trusting of Japanese companies.

Being already behind schedule by four years, it wasn't easy for us to look for South Korean companies that could newly produce the auto parts. Instead of working with Sanyo, we urgently asked around for companies that could produce batteries for us. As it happened, I met with the president of LG Chemical, which produced mobile phone batteries.

"The time is coming when automobile batteries will become more important. Therefore, I hope that LG will produce the batteries for our hybrid cars."

But the president of LG Chemical turned me down because production was unprofitable. In the end, LG Chemical produced the batteries only after Chairman Mong-Gu Chung stepped forward and persuaded LG's Chairman Bon-Moo Koo. We couldn't find a company to produce motors for us. As an alternative, we assigned the motor production to our subsidiary, Hyundai Mobis, and designed the motors ourselves.

However, realistically it was impossible to catch up with Toyota. Hyundai Motors finally developed a hybrid car six years after Toyota did. It was still a battle well fought, rather than floundering as a result of Toyota's obstruction. But neither the media and nor the public knew about this inside story. They could never imagine how intense the fight for survival is in the automobile industry in order to secure original technology before others do. They simply criticise Hyundai for not having foresight and for being tardy in developing hybrid cars.

Of course, the responsibility for formulating the wrong strategy ultimately rests with me. I've absolutely no intention of shirking this responsibility. And the more fundamental problem lay in the fact that we didn't possess the core technology. If we had possessed the original technology for core auto parts, it wouldn't have posed any threat to us, no matter how our competitors obstructed us. From then on, we devoted all our energies to localising the production of all major auto parts. I came to realise acutely how risky it was – in this competitive automobile business – to partner with companies from other countries.

This shows that our survival in the automobile business depends on the question of whether we possess our own technology or not. It's hard for a company that doesn't possess its own technology to survive this competition. I was keenly aware of the importance of possessing our own technology, having seen how the Hyundai Excel almost became unexportable because of Bosch, and how our development of hybrid cars was delayed because of Toyota's obstruction. Once again, I had learned the valuable lesson that we had to secure our own technology in our core business areas, no matter what.

Part 5

Driving the World with My Own Technology

I advise our engineers to spend fifty-one percent of their time in the company studying for themselves, and to spend the remaining forty-nine percent on the company. If every employee studies diligently and builds their competence, the company's competence will naturally catch up.

33

Now Let's Defeat Them Using Technology

When I was overseeing the research institute, the institute's yearly budget exceeded 2.5 trillion won (US$2.5 billion). Every day we spent around 10 billion won (US$10 million) of the budget. I had been given the job of deciding what to spend this budget on. If I spent the budget carelessly as a result of misjudgements, it could cause enormous damage for the entire company. I was in a position of great responsibility and power. To avoid making mistakes, I had to always agonise stressfully about the budget and how to execute it.

When South Korea's leading automobile companies went bankrupt, I inspected each company as the head of due diligence. This was so that Hyundai Motors could assess whether we could revitalise the companies if we decided to buy them out.

To tell the truth, all the while I was mulling over a question. These companies had been considerably larger and financially more robust than Hyundai had been when I first joined. But why was it inevitable that they should collapse, one after the other, while a company that had once been the smallest was growing into a global company?

I could vaguely guess why as I inspected the bankrupt companies thoroughly. The reason was simple. Executives who had no knowledge of technology had seized full authority over business management.

From the moment I had started developing our own engines, Chairman Ju-Yong Chung had given me full decision-making power over engine development. As the chairman of the company he proposed the direction for developing our own engines, but apart from that he entrusted all practical affairs to me – the engineer. Consequently, I had to independently decide on everything related to engine development, from practical affairs like engine design to budget execution. I could lead the research institute without major mistakes, because in every matter I made decisions based on my understanding of technology as an engineer.

But it wasn't so with other companies. Every important decision was made directly by management. The problem was that management made important decisions without adequately understanding technology. For instance, Company D decided that it was more profitable to buy technology from other countries than to invest time and money in developing its own technology as Hyundai had done. Company D would have to invest fully for at least five to six years if it wanted to develop its own technology, but it didn't feel the need to do so. For that reason, it imported all its core technology from abroad, purchasing engines from Australia and gearboxes from Germany. It was competitive initially, but later its production costs gradually rose. After analysing the production costs, we found that the costs of Company D's automobile engines and gearboxes were almost twice as much as Hyundai Motors's.

Yet it sold its automobiles more cheaply than Hyundai Motors. It was a wholly unprofitable business structure.

Company S was similar. Company S was importing engines and gearboxes from Benz, but the technology it was using was outdated technology that Benz had used twenty years before. But Company S had little choice but to buy that technology at a very costly price, and it was inevitable that its production costs grew as a result. In the end, it lost its competitiveness on the market.

It's hard to survive in the automobile industry without technological prowess. Yet the ultimate decision makers in these companies didn't understand the significance of technology, and they neglected investing in technology development.

Our society is slowly transforming into a technology-based society. In the business environment especially, it has become harder to even properly assess market trends without an understanding of technology. In particular, it's easy for management to make misjudgements if they don't have a proper understanding of technology, and in the end their companies will inevitably fall behind, no matter how outstanding they are. We can survive for long time only if we can assess the market accurately based on technology, and develop the needed technology one step ahead of the others.

34
Beautiful Days of My Life

I worked at Hyundai Motors for twenty-eight years, twenty-two of them as an executive. It's not an overstatement to say that I spent the prime of my life entirely at Hyundai. Sometimes people are surprised when I tell them that I worked at Hyundai for such a long time. That is because the strong and masculine corporate image of Hyundai and my own image are quite different. They wonder how someone like me, who has never once raised his voice, could survive in such a harsh organisation.

But I must confess that I wasn't a manager who was easy to deal with. I was promoted very quickly because I had carried out a core project – engine development – during a time when Hyundai Motors was growing rapidly. Perhaps my promotion was the fastest in the company's history. Consequently, my subordinates were always five or six years older than me. But they couldn't write me off, because I was a superior who won them over with my competence rather than with my position.

Since I started designing engines, I never made Hyundai's executives or Mitsubishi's engineers my competitors. From early on, I made Toyota's and Benz's heads of engine technology my competitors. I believed that I needed to compete with the world's top experts in order to develop abilities that were second to theirs.

In the same vein, I trained our engineers to be very strong. In the world of technology, we cannot settle for moderate efforts, because victors and vanquished are clearly divided. I believed that we couldn't fall short in any respect. Therefore, I pushed our team of engineers hard to create a team that possessed world-class technical skills. Fortunately, our engineers trusted and followed me. Our teamwork was remarkable. Whatever project we were given, we reached our objectives while working in perfect order, like one body. They researched late into the night if I instructed them to, and subsequently, even if I didn't instruct them to, they took it upon themselves and worked even harder. They had a difficult time, but at a certain point our team stood united, with the confidence that we were on par with any company in the world, just as we were in engine design.

It was the same in times of crisis. This happened when we were transferring the Theta engine technology to Benz. Chrysler suddenly intimated that it would be hard for them to use the Theta engine.

"The engine our company needs is a 2,400 cc model, so the Theta engine seems a little small. If you're unable to provide us with an alternative within the next four months, it'll be difficult for us to use the Theta engine."

We had originally designed the 1,800 cc, 2,000 cc and 2,200 cc models of the Theta engine. But Chrysler requested a 2,400 cc model, revealing its secret intention to reject our engine. At the time, Chrysler already had a plan to develop a 2,400 cc engine. Therefore, it gave us this excuse for rejecting the Theta engine.

I brooded over how I should respond to Chrysler's request. Increasing an engine's capacity from 2,200 cc to 2,400 cc wasn't a matter of simply increasing the engine displacement; it meant that we had to start working on the engine afresh, starting with the engine design. That was what Chrysler was after. It had given us that condition knowing that, no matter how brilliant our engine technology was, it would be difficult for Hyundai to develop a new engine in just four months.

But by nature, I don't like to give up without trying. Therefore, I convened our engineers right away. And I suggested that we find ways to produce the engine that Chrysler had requested in four months.

Four months later, our team had developed a 2,400 cc engine model, just as we had aimed to, and I told Chrysler to come and review the engine we had developed. But Chrysler wouldn't take my word for it until they visited our research institute. They assumed that we had called them after we had, at most, drawn a few designs. However, our team didn't only modify the Theta engine's design in four months. We presented them with a prototype, stripping away everything except the engine. Chrysler was astonished by our zeal. It could no longer make up excuses. Eventually, that was how the Theta engine became installed in Chrysler's automobiles as well.

Of course, it wasn't an easy task to develop a new engine in four months. Our engineers had to experience indescribable hardships as a result. But they trusted in my resolve to succeed in developing the new engine, and they followed my lead. I also trusted them and sought to help in any way I could. When I worked together with them, I felt that I was living in the way that suited me most. Looking back, I have never worked as energetically as I did during the days when I was absorbed in developing engines in the research lab, together with engineers who were more passionate and dedicated than any others. I'll remember those days as the most beautiful days of my life.

35

Teamwork That Transforms Crises into Opportunities

The reason I clashed with my direct superiors and executives after joining Hyundai Motors was that our views of technology were fundamentally different. Being clearly aware of what technological independence meant to an automobile company, I was adamant about developing our own technology no matter what. But most executives invariably disregarded the need to develop our own technology, and took buying technology from advanced companies for granted. They still had the same mindset about gearboxes, even after our engine technology had progressed beyond a certain level.

It happened right before I was promoted as the president of Hyundai Motors in 2005. Some board members had pushed for a technical partnership with an overseas company because they deemed our gearbox technology to be utterly dreadful.

It's a fact that our technical ability to design automatic gearboxes at the time wasn't particularly brilliant. We could design a five-speed gearbox, but not a six-speed gearbox. When that happened, our engineers did their best to raise our standard of technology as soon as possible. But there were board members who thought that it would be better to buy technology from other companies rather than to raise our own technical standards. Therefore, they formed a technical partnership with the German company ZF. ZF was recognised worldwide in the gearbox sector. Hyundai decided to jointly develop a six-speed gearbox with ZF and pay the company 150 billion won (US$150 million) in technical fees.

Then, a few months later, I was appointed president. I oversaw new technology and new products, and I had the opportunity to review past contracts. And then I discovered oddities when I was reviewing the contract with ZF. It was clearly stated in the contract that we had to pay 150 billion won in technical fees, but when I added up all the technical fees, including those specified in a dual contract, we actually had to pay as much as 450 billion won (US$450 million). It was evident that the contract would cause enormous damage to the company if it were enforced. Though gearbox technology was crucial, the conditions were excessive. Thinking that the problem was serious, I held multiple meetings with our engineers, and then went to Chairman Mong-Gu Chung right away.

"Chairman, isn't there a contract that you signed with ZF not long ago?"

"Yes, there is. I went all the way to Germany to sign it. Why?"

"I've reviewed the contract, and I think it's not right. If we go ahead with the contract as it is, we'll be in trouble for a long time in the future."

"What do you mean?"

"The technical fees that we must pay right now are a problem, but we'll also need to pay royalties per clause for a long time in the future, and each time it'll be a headache for us."

Chairman Mong-Gu Chung looked perplexed.

"I know what you mean, but what can we do about a contract that we've already signed?"

I replied, as if I had been waiting: "Chairman, if Hyundai wants to compete on the global market in the future, technological independence is of paramount importance. It'd be good to take this opportunity to become independent in cutting-edge gearbox technology."

I paused briefly, then stressed, "Please give me six months. I'll definitely find a way to resolve this problem."

Returning to my office after obtaining Chairman Mong-Gu Chung's permission, I wanted to rescind the contract at all costs. We didn't need an unfavourable contract that forced us to put up with enormous royalties because our technical standards were lacking. But I couldn't stubbornly break off a contract that had been signed between two companies. I had to somehow find a way out.

I gathered engineers who were veterans of the gearbox sector in my office. I explained the present situation and issued them with an order: "I'll give you guys six months. Use every means possible to develop the most suitable gearbox technology for Hyundai. No weekends and no rest days until we find the answer. Understand?"

Our engineers looked tense at what I had said. But they realised the significance of the matter, and they were keenly conscious of my belief that we had to take this opportunity to become independent in gearbox technology.

"Yes, sir."

A special task force was formed instantly. Our engineers had to develop the gearbox that we wanted in six months at all costs.

The concept of an automatic gearbox ultimately hinged upon the combination of the gears. It was our task to arrange the gears in diverse ways and look for the number of gears that could produce the speed we wanted. Seven of the research institute's most outstanding engineers repeated experiment after experiment, around the clock. They didn't leave the research institute, forfeited their weekends and shut themselves in the research lab, combining different gear sequences and repeating simulations. As a result of staying together and keeping up with our research, we could determine the gearbox combination we wanted after four months, faster than expected. I went to Chairman Mong-Gu Chung right away.

"Chairman, we found the answer. Now can we do without the contract with ZF?"

Chairman Mong-Gu Chung smiled broadly instead of replying. No executive would decline the opportunity to save 450 billion won in royalties.

Now only our negotiation with ZF remained. The job of cancelling a contract that had already been signed depended solely on my capability. I personally sent an email to ZF's chairman.

"Owing to unavoidable circumstances, we would like to terminate the gearbox contract which we have signed with your company. In return, we shall fully compensate for all the work that has been carried out so far. Please indicate the amount of compensation."

I had thought of compensating for the damage on reasonable terms and cancelling the contract. But ZF requested compensation of 30 billion won (US$30 million). I wrote a reply at once.

"You have requested compensation of 30 billion won, and we intend to fully compensate the amount, because it has been spent on Hyundai Motors. But we have also invested 30 billion won in this project, so we believe that we have the right to possess the relevant technology that we have invested in. Therefore, please send us the list of research work and expenses pertinent to the 30 billion won that your company has invested."

There was no reply from ZF for some time. Finally, the itemised statement arrived, but the amount it had invested, according to the statement, was less than 2.5 billion won (US$2.5 million). There wasn't much work that had been carried out, because the contract had been signed not long before. I wrote another reply.

"We have reviewed the itemised statement that your company has sent us. We shall fully compensate your company, as we have unintentionally terminated the contract. But we have decided that a compensation payment of 30 billion won is not reasonable. We intend to pay a total of 4 billion won in compensation, including 2.5 billion won for the expenses indicated in the itemised statement. If your company does not agree with this proposal, it is inevitable that we will conduct specific due diligence on the amounts indicated in the statement."

ZF eventually had no choice but to agree to my proposal. With that, the gearbox technical partnership that we had formed with ZF came to an end with a compensation payment of 4 billion won. We concluded the partnership by paying a hundredth of the 450 billion won that we had needed to pay when the contract was in effect.

However, what was more meaningful than rescinding an unfavourable contract was the fact that our team's ability to develop gearboxes progressed rapidly as a result. Our engineers could upgrade their previously inadequate technical skills in the field of gearbox technology, thanks to the in-depth research they had conducted in a short span of time. The technology that we developed independently for six-speed, eight-speed and ten-speed gearboxes in four months culminated in our possession of two hundred and thirty international patents. Above all, this was possible because our engineers possessed a bold spirit and passion, and devoted themselves to meeting the goals they were given. We could transform crises into opportunities because of our engineers' resolve and teamwork to achieve technological independence without depending on advanced companies.

36

More Terrifying Than an Enraged Superior

I was an executive for many years, and what I believed was most important was to raise up many engineers who were more competent and intelligent than me. For that to happen, I shared generously with my juniors what I knew, what I had experienced and what I had learnt throughout my life. And I always encouraged my juniors to surpass me. I believed that only then would our company grow and South Korea's automobile industry have a future.

But I was known as a merciless superior to employees who had no passion for their work. Perhaps that was why they used to say that they were most frightened when they came to report to me. Because I don't recklessly gloss over anything when giving my approval. When subordinates came to me for approval, I studied the documents meticulously and then questioned them on the spot concerning issues that I had questions about.

"This seems odd. How did this happen?"

Some employees would be flustered and unable to answer my questions right away. That was because they weren't entirely well informed about their work. When that happened, I lashed out at them without glossing over their work.

"How could you not have any opinion on work that has been assigned to you? Conduct proper research, then come back again with the correct reasoning."

On one occasion, when an executive I had sent away in that manner reported to me again, he brought along a line-up of his team members. He thought he might not be able to answer my incisive questions on his own, so he brought everyone along, including the department head, the deputy head and even the assistant manager. I berated him.

"You should study this on your own and organise your thoughts before coming. Why did you bring all your team members here? That's not what I want. I want to listen to your opinion, not the opinions of others. So please study your work. If this continues, how can I give you a good grade for your performance appraisal?"

That their performance will be reflected in their year-end performance appraisal is the most terrifying thing you can say to an office worker. That is because they cannot be promoted at the proper time if they don't fare well in their performance appraisal. Therefore, my subordinates had to study, as if it were a matter of life and death, to survive. In this way I created an atmosphere where employees were compelled to study independently. If they built their competence in this way, it would eventually be helpful to them, and the company would naturally thrive too. Hence, I used to advise our engineers to spend fifty-one percent of their time in the company studying for themselves, and to spend the remaining forty-nine percent on the company. That was because I believed that even if they spent only forty-nine percent of their time on the company, it was in the company's interest. If every employee studies diligently and builds their competence, the company's competence will automatically catch up.

Any organisation can become a thriving organisation only if the juniors perform better than the seniors. For that to happen, members of a company must share with one another the information that they have. When a piece of information passes through many hands and is reprocessed, the quality of that information increases, and competence is built. Therefore, I didn't tolerate employees who hid information on their desks and kept it to themselves. That was because I believed that information had to flow freely. Hyundai Motors could replicate periods of rapid growth over a short time span because I had first contributed my own advanced technical skills, and because it had a system where members of the company could share their information. The fact that numerous employees now leading Hyundai Motors are juniors with whom I used to work at the research institute is one of the things that make me proud.

37

My Special Mode of Communication

I was a superior who was fastidious to a fault when I received business reports, but I wasn't strict about the subordinate-superior relationship in every matter. I was very fond of spending time with my subordinates. I went hiking with them whenever I had time, and I made time to exercise with them during lunch. I trusted and loved my employees, who trusted and followed my lead, as if they were my family. Perhaps that was unsurprising, because they were people with whom I had built up trust as together we experienced objections from within the company and countless failures since the days we started developing our own engines.

Hyundai Motors stops all work at five o'clock on Wednesday afternoons. This is because it has become a company rule to stop work after five on that day. Even the engineers who have shut themselves in the research labs all stop working and rest.

I liked meeting the research institute's engineers at this time. Therefore, I used to host *samgyeopsal* parties on the lawn in front of the research institute every Wednesday.[7] Of course, by then

---

7 Translator's note – *Samgyeopsal* is a popular Korean dish of three-layered grilled pork belly meat.

our research institute had expanded to hundreds of departments and around ten thousand engineers. I couldn't meet them all at once, so I met four hundred of them from different departments each week. When I met each engineer face to face as we grilled meat and chatted candidly, I could naturally learn about their difficulties and troubles at work. Then, when the atmosphere was right, we played football on the lawn to relieve our pent-up stress.

Apart from researchers, our research institute also had around a thousand production employees, and I shared a close relationship with them as well. The production employees had a somewhat mischievous side, and I once held a barbeque party on a weekend to boost their morale.

There was an outdoor pool at the research institute. When they got excited, they grabbed me and threw me into the pool, which was more than two metres deep. It was mid-September then, so the water was rather cold. As I struggled out of the pool, they laughed and applauded, as if they were enjoying it. I realised that my glasses were missing only after I had come out of the pool. As soon as I told them that I had lost my glasses, they all rushed into the pool at once. Around sixty employees plunged into the pool at the same time and searched the floor of the pool thoroughly before they found my glasses. As a result, all of us ended up looking like drowned rats. It was so amusing that I still remember us pointing at one another and laughing for a good while.

I was ill with a cold on my way to Germany for a business trip the following day and felt miserable, but I believed that teamwork was formed through such togetherness. Our research institute's ten thousand engineers could demonstrate their formidable potential because they worked as one in this way.

My Special Mode of Communication

These days, we talk a lot about communication, but I think that communication is nothing special. Isn't communication about creating an atmosphere where we can speak to each other freely and face to face, and in the process build trust through which we can believe and depend on one another?

Because of these efforts, my subordinates were afraid of me on one hand and invariably trusted and followed me on the other. Even now that I've retired from Hyundai Motors, I can stay in contact and meet with the employees with whom I worked back then, because I treated them without inhibition as if they were my family and friends.

38

Achieving Miracles with One Heart and Mind

Hyundai Motors's trade union is famed for being very tough. Every year, intense negotiations are conducted between union members and management over wages. The views of union members and management inevitably differ, because their interests differ. Management has to act in the company's interests, and the union has to speak for the interests of union members. Therefore, negotiations often fall apart, and the union stages sit-ins. Perhaps this trade union played a role in how Hyundai earned its tough image.

I was one of the few executives who interacted freely with the union. That was in 1997, when I was transferred from the Mabuk Research Institute and appointed the director of Ulsan's automobile research institute. I was transferred to Ulsan's automobile research institute to improve the company's automobile technology, because the Mabuk Research Institute's engine development work had already reached a significant standard at the time.

On the first day of my new appointment, I reported to work in the morning, but hundreds of people were crowded at the entrance of the research institute. Upon enquiring what was happening, I was told that Ulsan's union members had all turned up to welcome me. That union members would turn up and welcome a newly appointed research institute director had never once happened since the company's inception. I couldn't drive them away, so I alighted from the car and shook everyone's hand as I walked into the research institute.

As a matter of fact, there had been an incident thanks to which I was perhaps receiving this warm reception. It had happened when I was the director of the Namyang Research and Development Centre. One day, the office manager of Ulsan's union, whom I knew, called me.

"Director, how have you been?"

"Oh, good. Manager, what's the matter?"

"Well… it's nothing… I heard that your younger brother is a renowned doctor. Is that right?"

"Well, yes. My younger brother is a doctor. But why do you ask? What's wrong?"

"Oh my, director, please help me."

Suddenly, I heard over the phone that he was on the verge of crying. After listening to his story, I learned that one of the union members at the Ulsan factory had been diagnosed with leukaemia. This member was also someone I knew well, because he had been aggressively involved in the labour movement. This friend had been hospitalised for three months after being diagnosed with leukaemia, but his condition hadn't improved at all.

"The doctor says his condition doesn't look promising. He's only twenty-nine years old, and I can't leave him to die, so I've called you out of desperation. Director, please help him."

I felt sorry for him, wondering how desperate he must have been to call me.

"My brother is a doctor, but he's a surgeon, so he won't be of much help to a leukaemia patient. But I'll find out, so wait a little while."

After ending the call, I phoned the haematology department at Asan Medical Center right away. A high school classmate of mine was working as department head at the hospital. After he heard the story, he said that it would be hard to help the man. I couldn't simply back off, so I asked again, desperately, "Is there really no way of helping him?"

Then he mumbled the end of his sentence: "There's one way, though…"

My ears pricked up.

"Is there? What's that?"

"The only way we can help your friend now is to hospitalise him and transfuse him with ten litres of fresh blood every day for forty-five days. But the blood must be very fresh, and it must be young blood that contains a large quantity of haematopoietic cells, which create new blood cells. Then he has a chance of getting better."

"Really? Then let's do that."

Right away, I called the union member who was suffering from leukaemia to Seoul and had him hospitalised at Asan Medical Center. I also requested help from the research institute's engineers. That was because back then, among the thousands of engineers working at our research institute, there was a considerable number of young engineers in their twenties and thirties. I told them the story, and gathered volunteers from those who had compatible blood types. Upon hearing the union member's pitiable story, the engineers too stepped forward to help, as if it were their own problem.

From that day on, a blood donation bus from Asan Medical Center started to visit our research institute every morning. The twenty engineers who had volunteered for that day donated their blood as soon as they came to work. After being transfused with fresh blood for the entire one and a half months, the union member miraculously recovered fully. It was literally a miracle that the research institute's engineers had achieved together, with one heart and mind.

The union members welcomed me warmly because I was appointed the director of Ulsan's research institute six months after that incident. The year I was transferred to Ulsan's research institute was the year of the currency crisis, so a significant number of employees had been dismissed. For that reason, union members took numerous disruptive actions, such as occupying the factories and attacking the offices of directors. But my office suffered absolutely no harm amid all that went on. Union members first turned up to keep vigil and protect my office. They then formed a team of six people in preparation for any unfortunate accident that might involve me, and escorted me wherever I went. I had simply done what I could, but because of what I had done, the union members accepted me without prejudice.

39

No Eternal Victor in the World of Technology

Three years ago, I moved to Doosan. I'm now overseeing the technology development of Doosan Group's subsidiaries in the tech sector, including Doosan Infracore, Doosan Heavy Industries, Doosan Electronics and Doosan Engine. When I was at Hyundai Motors, I presided over all practical affairs, from engine design to developing new automobiles; but at Doosan I oversee the future direction of the entire Doosan Group, and construct systems that are needed in the tech sector.

Doosan is the oldest company in South Korea. It has a history of no less than one hundred and eighteen years. But the company had focused on the consumer goods sector for most of its history before recently changing course to focus on technology-intensive industries, for instance developing power generators for heavy industry. Therefore, there are still areas of the company's core businesses where technical skills remain relatively weak. In order to improve Doosan's technical skills, I've been strengthening the company's systems, such as by pushing ahead with a general research institute as soon as I was appointed to my position.

I had been keenly aware when I was at Hyundai that a company's future hinged on technology, but I was even more conscious of this fact when I came to Doosan. If a company wants to succeed, it must first of all produce new products that apply new technology so as to gain competitiveness. For that to happen, the company requires the ability to predict future technology. I cannot guarantee Doosan's success simply because I contributed to growing Hyundai Motors into a global company. I can only prepare for the company's future with the insights I've gleaned as an engineer over the years.

In my office on the twenty-fifth storey of Doosan Tower, I conduct simulations to find out what new technologies might help the company gain competitiveness in the future and what kind of technology will create the largest ripple effects. The company will grow if these predictions hit the mark, and it's difficult to guarantee the company's future if they do not.

For manufacturing companies like Hyundai and Doosan, the recent growth of Chinese companies is very menacing. Chinese companies are investing fully in technology and catching up with us at a terrifying pace.

There's no other way to defeat them except to run faster than the speed at which China is keeping up with us. That was exactly the strategy I used at Hyundai Motors – to assess technological trends accurately and decide on strategies that would allow me to stay a step ahead of rival companies. And to recruit as many competent engineers as possible, and create an environment where they could work with ease.

These days, it's also imperative in the engineering sector to understand the convergence of technologies. In the past, companies in the manufacturing sector could gain competitiveness by possessing only mechanical technology. But now it's hard to gain competitiveness if we don't integrate IT and communications technology. As technology becomes more complex and products more diverse, we must also respond appropriately to the demands of customers who have become more fastidious. In today's business environment, it's hard to close the gap if we are one step behind.

For that reason, recent companies have been pouring their heart and soul into hiring CEOs with a background in engineering. The fact that more than half of the CEO positions in South Korea's hundred largest companies are filled by people who have a background in science and engineering reflects this reality. The percentage of CEOs who have a background in science and engineering, which was merely forty-five percent ten years ago, has tipped and now stands at sixty percent. This is because it's now difficult to operate businesses without any understanding of technology in a business environment where technological trends are quickly changing and becoming more complex.

In the past, the paramount task for engineers of my generation was to catch up with advanced technology as quickly as possible. But there is never an eternal victor in the world of technology. Just as we caught up with advanced technology, there are rival companies that are catching up with us with terrifying vigour.

The next-generation engineers must take the lead in technology without being caught up by rival companies, and create new markets using innovative thinking. It's tough now for engineers to remain experts only in their fields of expertise. They must understand the associated technology, and possess a deep and broad technological understanding. Only engineers who possess the acumen to respond swiftly to a different business environment and the ability to forecast future technology can lead the society of the future.

Epilogue
Engineers Influence Millions of Lives

In May 2011, I was at a graduation ceremony at the State University of New York. Before me were seated around three thousand four hundred graduates who were about to take their first steps into the world, and six thousand parents. Hope for the future and youthful vigour overflowed on the faces of the graduates. As I looked at each of their faces, I felt as if I had returned to my youth of thirty-eight years before. Back to my twenties, when I went abroad to study without a definite plan, having decided to study the engine technology of developed countries. The day when I stepped into this campus for the first time remained vivid, as if it were only yesterday.

I rehearsed in my mind my speech to the graduates, which I had corrected and revised multiple times. There was only one thing I wished to tell them.

"Challenge yourself to become the best!" I emphasised to the young adults who were stepping into the world.

"This generation is now pursuing materialistic values more than any other generation in the past. Everyone wants viable opportunities and stable jobs. Unfortunately, talented individuals who desire to seize new opportunities to challenge themselves are rare. But I believe that talented individuals who undertake challenges, especially in this generation, will prove their real worth. Just as I ventured against the objections of countless people and developed our own automobile engine thirty years ago."

When my seven-minute speech ended, the graduates responded with thunderous applause. That day, the State University of New York recognised my services as an engineer and awarded me with an honorary doctorate, as well as appointing me to an endowed professorship. I was the first South Korean to be honoured with this professorship.

The graduation ceremony ended, and for the first time in a long while I walked the streets of New York with my wife. The streets of New York had changed beyond recognition from thirty-eight years before. It wasn't difficult to spot automobiles bearing the Hyundai logo on the streets. This showed that the stature of South Korea's automobile brands had risen.

This reality warmed my heart. I felt that it had been recognised that the challenges I had undertaken hadn't been in vain. Around that time I was ranked the sixteenth most influential figure in the automobile industry around the world. Of course, this wasn't an outcome that I had achieved by my own efforts. It would have been impossible without the hard work of the engineers with whom I had laboured together, by the sweat of our brows.

The achievements that South Korea's first-generation engineers have made over the years are remarkable. Though we started out in the automobile industry more than a hundred years later than other countries, South Korea has become the world's fifth largest car-producing country. Perhaps this is why South Korean engineers, who have made waves in the automobile and semiconductor industries, are highly valued these days even in overseas countries.

There are only six countries competing in the global automobile industry with their own brands: the United States, Japan, South Korea, Germany, France and Italy. Apart from South Korea, the other countries produced aircraft during the Second World War. Needless to say, their engine technology is outstanding. On the other hand, during the Second World War, South Korea was a country where it was hard to catch a glimpse of an automobile, much less an aircraft. It's astonishing that a country like ours has acquired world-class technical skills in such a short span of time. Perhaps this is why foreign engineers are curious to know exactly what kind of people South Korean engineers are that they could achieve this success story, creating something out of nothing.

I once spoke with some first-generation engineers about this. But our conclusion was that we hadn't made these achievements because South Korean engineers were especially outstanding or intelligent. Nor do I think that we could develop our own engines because we had more experience in engine design and were smarter than Toyota's or Honda's engineers. I think that we could succeed only because we constantly challenged ourselves without being afraid of failing, because we pushed ahead tenaciously without despairing after failing once or twice, and because we were backed by the strong support of our company's executives.

I'd like to say this to those who dream of becoming the next Steve Jobs or Bill Gates: judges determine the lives and deaths of scores of people throughout their lives, doctors impact on the lives of thousands, but engineers influence the lives of millions.

When a person's wonderful imagination is made into a product, this product goes onto the market and exerts an influence that is a hundred or a thousand times greater. As a result, we can lead comfortable and productive lives that were previously unthinkable. Just as we are now living in a world that was completely unimaginable before Steve Jobs introduced the smartphone.

No doubt the environment that future engineers find themselves in will be quite different from the one our first-generation engineers experienced. Our generation's aim was to catch up as quickly as possible with the leading technical skills of developed countries. At least the goal we had to work towards was clear. But it will be different for future engineers. They must lead the world in new ways that no one has anticipated. For that reason, they must keep up with technological changes that occur faster over time. They must also understand the convergence of diverse technologies. Most of all, they must trailblaze new markets using innovative thinking.

Nevertheless, I hope that our young people will dream big and embrace challenges fearlessly. I hope you won't feel intimidated by the world, and that you will explore your own potential ambitiously. As someone who walked the engineer's path before you did, I sincerely root for your future, which is filled with infinite possibilities.

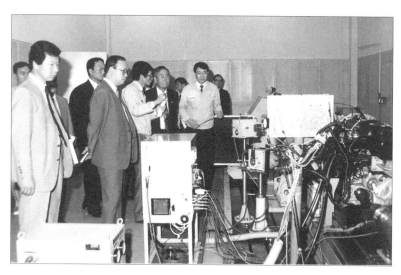

(Top) Minister of Science and Technology Jin-Hyeon Kim's visit to the Mabuk Research Institute in 1990. (Bottom) Our research lab at the Mabuk Research Institute in 1990.

(Top) Mitsubishi Chairman Kubo's visit to the Mabuk Research Institute in 1990. (Bottom) At a party to celebrate the mass production of the Alpha engine in 1991.

With Bosch's vice president Peter Tyroller at a meeting with Bosch board members in 2007.

(Top) The partnership-signing ceremony between Hyundai Motors and Microsoft in 2008. (Bottom) I received the Best Chief Technology Officer Award from the Korea Industrial Technology Association in 2008.

(Top) The Tau engine received WardsAuto's Top Ten Best Engines Award in 2008. (Bottom) With Hyundai Motors's executives at the WardsAuto ceremony.

(Top and bottom) The Hyundai Genesis received the 2009 award for North American Car of the Year at the North American International Auto Show in Detroit.

(Top) With Hyundai Motors executives at a banquet hosted by the Korea Society in 2009. (Bottom) The awards ceremony for South Korea's Top Hundred Technologies and Leaders in 2010.

(Top) I was awarded the Grand Prize at the thirteenth National Academy of Engineering of Korea awards ceremony in 2009. (Bottom) A briefing session on the development of electric vehicles at the Blue House in 2010.

The Doosan Tech Forum in 2013.

Alpha Engine

The Alpha engine was South Korea's very first original engine, developed in 1991. It was installed in the Hyundai Scoupe. The Alpha II engine was subsequently developed in 2005 after several aspects of the Alpha engine were improved, including its fuel efficiency.

Theta Engine

Developed in 2002, the Theta engine was installed in the Hyundai NF Sonata. The engine's technology was exported to countries like Japan and the United States, and the engine helped South Korea leapfrog into a front runner position in the automobile industry. It was the single most produced engine in a year, and its production record hasn't yet been broken.

Tau Engine

The Tau engine was developed in 2008. It received the WardsAuto Award, the most prestigious award in the engine sector, for its high performance, high engine displacement and high fuel efficiency. Moreover, in 2009 the Hyundai Genesis, which was fitted with the Tau engine, was the very first vehicle in South Korea to be selected as the North American Car of the Year.

HARRIETT PRESS

Bridging Cultures with Stories

Harriett Press is a Singapore boutique publishing and translation company founded in 2018. We are on a mission to publish high-quality English translations of relevant, inspirational and influential Asian literature, and to make them accessible to English-speaking readers worldwide. We are constantly searching for distinctive voices and stories that will uplift, challenge and empower readers. We combine exceptional literary standards with artistic designs to enrich the experience of reading books in translation. We also provide quality translation and interpretation services, and conduct translation workshops for students and emerging translators.

Follow us to stay updated on our latest news:
harriettpress.com
facebook.com/sgharriettpress
instagram.com/harriettpress